M. Gete

Literacy
and Learning
Lessons

From a Longtime Teacher

Regie Routman

INTERNATIONAL
 Reading Association
800 BARKSDALE ROAD, PO BOX 8139
NEWARK, DE 19714-8139, USA
www.reading.org

The International Reading Association attempts, through its publications, to provide a forum for a wide spectrum of opinions on reading. This policy permits divergent viewpoints without implying the endorsement of the Association.

Executive Editor, Publications   Shannon Fortner

Acquisitions and Developmental Editor   Tori Mello Bachman

Managing Editor   Christina M. Terranova

Editorial Associate   Wendy Logan

Design and Composition Manager   Anette Schuetz

Design and Composition Associate   Lisa Kochel

Project Editor   Renée Brosius

Cover   Design, Lise Holliker Dykes; Photograph, Chuck Fazio

The publisher would appreciate notification where errors occur so that they may be corrected in subsequent printings and/or editions.

Library of Congress Cataloging-in-Publication Data

Routman, Regie.
  Literacy and learning lessons from a longtime teacher / Regie Routman.
    p. cm.
  Includes bibliographical references and index.
  ISBN 978-0-87207-479-8
1. Language arts. 2. Effective teaching. 3. Motivation in education. I. Title.
  LB1576.R7577 2012
  372.6--dc23
                          2012023946

Suggested APA Reference

Routman, R. (2012). *Literacy and learning lessons from a longtime teacher*. Newark, DE: International Reading Association.

For teachers, who work tirelessly to transform
students' literacy and learning lives

Contents

Acknowledgments   viii

About the Author   ix

Introduction   1

1. It's all about relationships 5
2. Acknowledge our colleagues 6
3. Infuse purpose and authenticity into all we do 7
4. Create a beautiful and meaningful environment 9
5. Ensure that the heart and mind go together 11
6. Ask more vital questions 12
7. Build a strong foundation 14
8. Apply an optimal learning model 15
9. Read professionally 16
10. Plan with the end in mind 17
11. Do more demonstrations 19
12. Bond with our students and colleagues 21
13. Instill determination to learn 22
14. Provide more choice within structure 23
15. Aim to develop self-determining learners 24
16. Teach rereading 26
17. Share our best ideas 28
18. Put guided reading in perspective 29
19. Examine our management focus 31
20. Seek to do better 33
21. Become an active listener 34
22. Reward persistence 36
23. Focus on the writer first and the writing second 38
24. Expect more 40
25. Read aloud every day 41
26. Treat all members of the school community respectfully 43
27. Connect writing with reading 44
28. Celebrate learners' strengths 46

29. Be a reader 47
30. Implement standards thoughtfully 48
31. Make certain students are engaged, not just on-task. 50
32. Integrate word study across the curriculum. 51
33. Imagine the possibilities 53
34. Observe an excellent kindergarten teacher 54
35. Take time to reflect. 56
36. Form unlikely friendships 58
37. Recognize that all learners have special needs 60
38. Choose and use excellent texts 61
39. Make no assumptions 62
40. Support English-language learners 64
41. Create a need to know 66
42. Enjoy teaching 68
43. Write more short pieces. 70
44. Use technology judiciously. 71
45. Do more frontloading 73
46. Acknowledge an unexpected hero 75
47. Teach with a sense of urgency. 77
48. Embrace public writing conferences 78
49. Provide feedback that supports the learner. 80
50. Read and write more texts. 82
51. Focus on the essential ingredients 84
52. Teach less, learn more 85
53. Expect correct spelling and conventions 86
54. Resist teaching to the test 88
55. Remain hopeful 90
56. Design and assign appropriate homework 91
57. Share inspiring stories. 93
58. Eliminate distractions 94
59. Teach handwriting 96
60. Collaborate more 97
61. Slow down to hurry up 98
62. Use simple rubrics. 99
63. Expect change 100
64. Apply whole-part-whole teaching 101
65. Live an interesting life. 103
66. Put the language in their ears 104

67. Aim for seamless teaching. 106
68. Nurture vocabulary development. 107
69. Rely on shared writing 109
70. View celebration as teaching 111
71. Establish a rich and relevant classroom library 112
72. Reduce the need for intervention. 114
73. Tell the truth 115
74. Ensure excellent first instruction for *all* students 117
75. Make students less dependent on us 119
76. Establish routines and rituals. 120
77. Be a leader as well as a team member. 122
78. Esteem every learner 123
79. Use common sense. 124
80. Do more shared reading 125
81. Put energy where results are most likely 127
82. Promote significant conversations 129
83. Develop shared beliefs 131
84. Make professional development our priority 133
85. Create access to complex texts. 135
86. Make parents our partners. 137
87. Assess as we teach 138
88. Promote oral language development 140
89. Advocate for saner practices 142
90. Be efficient. 144
91. Depend on formative assessment. 145
92. Build stamina. 147
93. See our classrooms through students' eyes 148
94. Know important literacy research. 150
95. Emphasize nonfiction—along with fiction. 152
96. Infuse the arts into teaching and learning. 154
97. Do more student-directed, small-group work 156
98. Rely on one-on-one reading conferences 158
99. Promote more opportunities for speaking. 160
100. Teach students, not standards 162
      A call to action 163

References   165

Index   167

Acknowledgments

Grateful thanks to project editor Renée Brosius, who enthusiastically supported the book's concepts and content from start to finish and who gave timely and useful feedback. Talented fifth-grade teacher Laurie Espenel thoughtfully read and responded to all the lessons, put her stamp of approval on them, and offered many wise suggestions. Thank you, Laurie! To my colleagues who offered encouragement and advice—you know who you are—heartfelt thanks. To my dear family and friends, as always, I count on your support and you never let me down. Finally, thanks to all the educators I have collaborated with in many schools over many years and with whom I continue to learn so much.

About the Author

 egie Routman is a national teacher and author with more than four decades of teaching, coaching, and leading in the United States and Canada. Her many books, journal articles, and resources provide clarity, support, specific demonstrations, and practical guidance to educators so they can teach reading and writing in a manner that is not only consistent with research and learning theory but also respectful of all students' needs, interests, and abilities. Her current work involves weeklong school residencies where she demonstrates effective literacy teaching in diverse classrooms, coaches teachers and principals, and facilitates ongoing professional conversations, all as a catalyst for sustainable, whole-school change. To replicate that work in many more schools and districts, she created *Regie Routman in Residence* (2008b, 2008c, 2009)—three groundbreaking, video-based professional development projects. See, also, www.regieroutman.org for her professional development offerings, most recent publications, and supportive resources for exemplary teaching and leading. See www.regieroutman.com for information on her Heinemann professional books and resources.

In addition, Regie sponsors a Teacher Recognition Grant through the International Reading Association. The annual $2,500 award honors an outstanding elementary classroom teacher dedicated to improving the teaching and learning of reading and writing. At least 60% of the school's students must be eligible for free or reduced-cost lunch. For complete information, see www.reading.org/Resources/AwardsandGrants/teachers_routman.aspx

In 2010, Regie became the first winner of the Sandra Kim Literacy Legacy Award sponsored by the Literacy for Special Needs Program at Seattle University in Seattle, Washington, USA, where she lives. Regie can be reached at regieroutman@gmail.com.

Introduction

Teaching today is as challenging as ever. Implementation of the latest standards, new evaluation measures, ongoing pressures to raise achievement, and the politics of literacy make our jobs extremely demanding. Still, there are some basic and unchanged factors we often can control. Wanting to do right by our students, ensuring they become fully literate, and giving them access to a rich and satisfying life of unparalleled opportunities remain some key reasons we educators continue to give our all. If we are knowledgeable, savvy, and willing, we do have the wherewithal to enrich and empower not just our students' literacy and learning lives but our own as well. After 45 years of teaching, leading, and coaching in diverse classrooms and schools, I have consolidated my thinking into what I believe to be the most significant lessons that lead to high success for all learners. These 100 lessons have evolved from my ongoing teaching, assessing, planning, coaching, leading, collaborating, researching, studying, reflecting, innovating, and living my life. In short, the lessons reflect my best professional advice after a lifetime of teaching and learning.

While lots of these topics have been discussed in my previous books and resources, in this latest book I refine and strengthen my instructional beliefs and practices, distilling them down to the essence of what's most important. Many of the lessons are entirely new and are based on my current thinking and actions around reading and writing, professional growth, and whole-school achievement. The book is an easy and relaxing read. One reader commented, "It's like sitting back and having a conversation with a friend." Knowing how little time we educators have to read and to study, the book is meant to be a go-to guide for inspiration, practical ideas, and specific, step-by-step teaching actions that have been proven to work with all students—struggling, gifted, special needs, English-language learners. Although the book is meant to be read from beginning to end, you can read and reread the lessons in any order that suits you. Use the book as a handy desktop reference, book study at a school, course to reenergize as a professional, process for improving our teaching, or gift to preserve, new, and experienced teachers. The book is intended for K–12 educators of all disciplines and specialties. Regardless of the content we teach, literacy is the foundational prerequisite that is every teacher's responsibility.

A bit of professional background: I have been a teacher and teacher–researcher since the mid-1980s when my first book, *Transitions: From Literature to Literacy*, was published. I wrote the book to show what was possible for underserved and underachieving students—in this case, African American students—who were not learning to read with their steady diet of basal reading selections and isolated skills supported by a proliferation of worksheets. Given wonderful children's literature as reading texts, the daily opportunity to write on self-selected topics, explicit teaching of phonics and other strategies, and lots of time and guidance to practice and apply what was authentically being taught, students soared as readers and writers. I went on to write many more books, all with the same intent—that is, to make literacy and learning lives better, easier, joyful, and more authentic and effective for students, teachers, principals, coaches, and families. *Transitions* (1988) was followed by *Invitations: Changing as Teachers and Learners K–12* (1990, 1994), *The Blue Pages* (1994), *Literacy at the Crossroads: Crucial Talk About Reading, Writing, and Other Teaching Dilemmas* (1996), *Conversations: Strategies for Teaching, Learning, and Evaluating* (2000), *Kids' Poems: Teaching Students to Love Writing Poetry* (2000), *Reading Essentials: The Specifics You Need to Teach Reading Well* (2003), *Writing Essentials: Raising Expectations and Results While Simplifying Teaching* (2005), and *Teaching Essentials: Expecting the Most and Getting the Best From Every Learner, K–8* (2008).

My first comprehensive resource for facilitating whole-school change, *Regie Routman in Residence: Transforming Our Teaching* (2008, 2009) www.regieroutman .com/inresidence/, is a literacy-based and video-based embedded professional development series centered on the reading/writing connection, writing for audience and purpose, and reading to understand. These virtual residencies are designed for school-based professional learning communities and grew out of my ongoing work in diverse schools. Recognizing that teachers and principals needed to observe what effective and efficient teaching and learning "look like" and "sound like" day by day, on site and in-depth, I created in the late 1990s a weeklong residency model, which I follow to this day and which continues to greatly inform and enrich my current thinking, beliefs, and practices. Working primarily in K–6 classrooms and schools with large populations of students who qualify for free and reduced-cost meals, many of whom are also English-language learners, I take over instruction for a week in two designated classrooms and—with teachers and the principal at the school observing—apply an Optimal Learning Model of demonstration teaching, shared experiences, and guided and independent practice. The end goal is to lead and coach teachers and students to become self-determining learners—that is, active learners who eventually have the knowledge, competence, and confidence to thoughtfully problem solve, responsibly innovate, and set their own worthwhile course that often goes beyond themselves to accomplish a "greater good." Most of the lessons in *Literacy and Learning Lessons From a Longtime Teacher* arise from my residency work.

In many ways, not much has changed since I began teaching more than four decades ago. Then, as now, authentic and purposeful teaching and texts have engaged and invigorated students and teachers. Also, while many students thrive in our schools, far too many still lag behind their peers. Debates continue over solutions, programs, and "best" methods to reach and teach all students. Yet for all the good intentions, efforts, and combined billions of dollars that have poured into initiatives to raise achievement, such as No Child Left Behind, Race to the Top, and the Common Core State Standards, it is likely that such initiatives will continue to yield mixed results. The only thing we know for certain that positively affects and sustains student achievement is the highly knowledgeable and effective teacher. Better yet is the highly effective teacher who is supported by strong leadership and a collaborative school culture. Achievement starts with focusing on our students and putting all the "issues" aside, as best we can. Regardless of their circumstances, our students come to us with the unspoken promise of developing fully realized literate and learning lives. My hope is that *Literacy and Learning Lessons From a Longtime Teacher* may provide you the impetus, knowledge, specifics, and determination to help meet that promise for all our students. To you, my esteemed colleagues, my hope is that you also enjoy the lifelong learning journey.

—Regie Routman
June 2012

It's all about relationships

More than any other factor in schoolwide achievement, the way people in a school relate to each other determines the success of the students, teachers, and principal. A school needs a healthy culture, ongoing collaboration, and a deep respect and regard for others in order for all members of the school community to thrive.

How do we establish those crucial trusting and caring relationships? A principal recently asked me for advice on how to be successful in her first year in a new school. "It's all about relationships," I told her. "Celebrate teachers' and students' strengths every day, get to know your staff as people, earn their trust, respect confidentiality, and don't make major changes right away." For any of us who work in schools, or in any organization, we have greater opportunities for growth when we can freely and joyfully collaborate with colleagues. This is no easy task. It requires accepting that every person has a different perspective and way of thinking; that respecting and valuing colleagues' views, talents, and background are a necessity for developing trust; and that gossip is not conversation.

The first thing I do when I am working in a school is to try to get to know the people—the teachers, specialists, office staff, and students. In a recent visit to a school, during our "working" lunch, the principal, curriculum director, and literacy coach each had a notebook in hand. I know they were surprised when I said, "Let's not work through lunch. Let's take a well-deserved break and just enjoy our time together." We wound up talking about our families, hobbies, cooking, and favorite things to do and eat. At the end of the lunch, I felt closer to each one of them. We had lots of laughs, learned about each other's lives, and knew each other better.

We simply cannot underestimate the power of positive relationships on the health, well-being, and achievement of all school community members. Without excellent relationships between students and teachers, teaching teams at and across grade levels, teachers and administrators, and students and their families, it's difficult to raise and sustain achievement and have a thriving school culture.

Acknowledge our colleagues

Look for ways to identify and comment on something a colleague has done well. Honest compliments build trust, and high-trust organizations are more likely to be collaborative and high achieving. Thoughtful gestures matter. Recognizing our colleagues' strengths results in a more robust learning culture. When we feel personally and professionally valued, we are apt to be happier, more productive, and more likely to take risks as teachers and learners.

Take action

- **Express appreciation specifically and often**. Most of us do not hear often enough that our efforts are valued. For example, thank a colleague who has shared a successful lesson, opened up his or her classroom for colleagues to observe, offered support to a new teacher, or raised an important schoolwide issue in a positive way.

- **Remember colleagues' birthdays**, special occasions, and individual accomplishments with a personal congratulation, short note, e-mail, text message, or card.

- **Publicly acknowledge a colleague's achievement in a staff meeting**. Or, before a scheduled professional development meeting, ask a peer to bring or share a student work sample, lesson plan, class-authored book, or anything outstanding we have noticed. Not only is a colleague's work publicly celebrated, but also we all benefit from learning about the excellent idea.

- **Perform acts of kindness each day**. For example, listen without judgment to a colleague who has had a tough day; volunteer to pick up a colleague's class from a special activity; share a lunch with a teacher who has forgotten his or her own or had no time to bring one. For a colleague who is not a good speller, offer to read a newsletter before it goes home to families.

Infuse purpose and authenticity into all we do

Making our teaching as authentic and purposeful as possible makes it much more likely that we engage and motivate all learners. When students understand and value the "what" of curriculum and standards, they are willing to invest in the "how." When they don't see the relevance of the lesson or activity, many make minimal efforts and even shut down. The first questions I ask students in a residency are, "Why am I here?" "Why does this matter?" and "Why are all the teachers observing?" Most often, students don't know. If we want students to invest full energy into their schoolwork, they must see the work as important to their lives in some way. A growing body of research confirms that the more authentic and meaningful our instruction is, the greater gains students make. One example is the use of real-world nonfiction materials (Duke, Caughlan, Juzwik, & Martin, 2012). Always we need to remain flexible in our instruction and be guided by the questions, "What do students need to succeed in doing?" and "What's the most authentic way to teach it?" Being flexible and teaching authentically include being willing and able to change course and modify our instruction based on the immediate needs of our students, which must always take priority over our lesson plan. In fact, changing plans mid-course may prove to be more valuable to student learning than the lesson we originally planned.

Take action

- ◆ **Ask ourselves constantly, "Why does this activity matter for students?"** For example, doing a picture walk for every guided reading lesson in the primary grades, whisper reading for every guided reading lesson in the intermediate grades, preteaching most vocabulary, following a predetermined sequence for teaching skills, and so on.

- ◆ **State the purpose and goals** of every lesson, task, activity, or change of plan. Say something like, "Here's why you need to know this...," "The reason I'm thinking out loud is...," "We'll be working in small groups today to try out and practice...before you attempt it on your own," or "We're going to change our plan for today because I noticed.... Here's why that's important, and here's what we'll be doing next."

♦ **Have students wrestle with real-world issues** by—with our guidance—reading, discussing, and writing about relevant and complex topics and ideas in social studies, science, politics, health, the arts, and more with real-world texts and resources. Make every effort to provide firsthand experiences and to personalize required curriculum study to students' lives, cultures, and backgrounds.

♦ **Write and publish for authentic audiences and purposes**. My experience and teacher research confirm that this is the single most important factor for having students invest their full energies into composing, revising, and editing (see pp. 11, 17–18, 70 and *Transforming Our Teaching Through Writing for Audience and Purpose*, Routman, 2008b).

♦ **Question the use of inauthentic resources**, such as worksheets on isolated skills, senseless activities in adopted programs, and the overuse and overreliance on test preparation materials.

Create a beautiful and meaningful environment

We spend most of our days as teachers and leaders in a classroom, office, or school building. Those spaces serve as our home away from home. Work with our students and colleagues to make our spaces as attractive, organized, and peaceful as possible. A beautiful and useful space not only lifts our spirits; but it also is an excellent public relations vehicle for showing off our literacy and learning community.

Take action

- **Group desks in clusters** so students can collaborate, at least some of the time. Consider adding lamps and comfortable seating, such as pillows, to the reading or book corner. Add a plant or two to personalize and enliven our space.

- **Involve students in organizing and setting up the classroom library**, and give them choices in the types of texts, genres, series, and authors they prefer. Work out a checkout system with students so they can manage it. Have book titles, including student-authored work, facing outward for easy access and browsing (see *Reading Essentials*, Routman, 2003, for more information).

- **Make sure that displayed work, word walls, and charts are legible and accessible** throughout the school—posted at students' eye level, written in language students understand, useful as a student resource, clear in purpose to potential readers, and accurate in facts, format, spelling, and grammar.

- **Determine what certain bulletin boards might emphasize**, such as developing classroom and school rules, posting important resources, and creating charts and rubrics with students that are based on finding out what students know, are learning, and are expected to apply.

- **Aim for having most posted work in rooms and hallways created by students with teacher guidance.** Walls covered with commercially made charts impart an impersonal look and feel. Think about having students make borders for bulletin boards—based on the alphabet, math patterns, class raps, and so forth—and hand write or word process class-generated charts.

- **Explain posted writing** so that the audience and purpose of writing featured in school hallways is clear and will be read by students, teachers, and visitors. Compose a paragraph with students to explain the background, content, and goals of the posted writing. Otherwise, many posted pieces become just artifacts and are not read or appreciated.

- **Make certain that posted work throughout the school is focused on learning** across the curriculum and celebrating students' accomplishments, rather than on management behaviors and rules.

Ensure that the heart and mind go together

Do whatever we can to first capture students' and teachers' hearts before worrying about how much we are teaching them. Have you noticed that no one ever says "mind and heart?" That's because if we win a person's heart, the engagement and effort of the mind is more likely to follow. To reach the heart, we appeal to people's interests and needs, respect their culture and background, value them as individuals, and care about their well-being. As an example, when teaching writing I know that if I can engage students' hearts in an authentic topic and audience that matters to them, I can teach them everything they need to know about writing—organization, elaboration, grammar, revision, editing, and so on—and they will willingly do the hard writing work. However, without that heart–mind connection, writing efforts will often be lackluster and minimal.

Take action

- **Get to know students and colleagues**—their backgrounds, interests, and families—by welcoming and encouraging their stories, customs, hobbies, and unique characteristics.

- **Let the people we spend time with every day know we value them**—through caring actions, verbal comments, facial expressions, short notes, kind gestures, and thoughtfulness in all we do.

- **As much as we can, make students' interests central to our curriculum** through the projects we assign, reading materials in our classroom and school libraries, choices of writing topics, and respect we show for their talents, differences, and needs.

Ask more vital questions

The questions we pose to students and ourselves say a lot about our instruction, level of classroom discourse, expectations for students, and the depth of our knowledge about teaching and learning. We need to be responsive to what students are attempting to do and say as well as to what they are and are not learning. By continuously assessing, mostly through asking probing questions while we are teaching, we can adjust and tailor our instruction to better meet students' needs, interests, and our required curriculum and standards. Do not immediately jump in when students "don't know." Let them come to know, through relevant questioning, additional teaching, and scaffolding that we will support them to figure out their own "answers." In addition, students who develop a mind-set of self-monitoring, problem solving, self-questioning, and goal setting are more likely to do well on standardized tests, as they have internalized and can independently apply the habits of successful readers, writers, and thinkers.

Take action

- ◆ **Ask more open-ended questions that require students to think more deeply**, find evidence in a text, and ponder possible solutions:

  - "What do you notice?"
  - "Can you say more about that?"
  - "What makes you think that?"
  - "Where does it say that?"
  - "What's another way you could say that?"
  - "How else could you figure that out?"

- ◆ **Request that a colleague observe a lesson and write down the questions asked of students**. Self-evaluate. Check that most of our questions are not just about management and literal-level thinking and that we are asking important questions that lead to deeper thinking and learning.

- ◆ **Aim for students to eventually self-question** and self-direct the inner questioning that is a hallmark of thoughtful learners:

- "Do I need to reread this to be sure it makes sense?"
- "Can I figure out the meaning of the unknown word by reading the sentences that come before and after it?"
- "Is my writing lead good enough, or should I rewrite it?"
- "Is this paper ready to hand in? Have I checked it thoroughly so it's clear, legible, and has my best spelling and conventions?"

With demonstrations, shared experiences, and guided practice, even primary-grade students can be taught to ask—and answer—their own significant questions, such as those for guided reading groups, literature conversations, small-group work, peer talk, independent work, and self-evaluations.

Build a strong foundation

When Frank, my husband, designed a tree house for our two granddaughters, putting in a strong foundation proved to be the most problematic and time-consuming issue. The designated space was at a high elevation, set back in a wooded area. Getting up to the area required going up a narrow, winding path, which made it impossible to bring in heavy equipment. The foundation had to be cleared and dug entirely by hand. Luckily, we found a strong-bodied and willing young man to do the work. Day by day, and over several weeks, he was undeterred by the heavy clay soil, big rocks, branches, tree roots, and very slow progress. He knew that without a solid foundation, deliberately built for the long run, the structure might be fine for a while but, inevitably, cracks and other problems would surface and need to be fixed.

So it is with our teaching. A quick fix over a weak foundation just delays the necessary digging in, all the way down to the roots and clearing away of dead wood. We must do the hard, foundational work—slow and plodding as it is—in order to become highly competent. Without that foundation of deep literacy and content knowledge along with the routines and craft of effective teaching, we are essentially powerless to respond thoughtfully to the latest trends, mandates, resources, and research. We are easy prey for publishers, naysayers, and opportunists outside and inside the educational field. We simply cannot advocate for needed change and make wise instructional decisions—long term, day by day, and moment to moment—without an unshakable, solid foundation of informed beliefs and practices about teaching, learning, assessing, and leading. We won't know the important questions to ask, the best practices to apply, the resources that will best support us. The educational pendulum will always swing, but we must not. Once we become highly knowledgeable, we may shift a bit to the right or left, based on relevant research and experiences, but if our foundation is rock solid, the shift will be an intentional, well-informed movement and not a full tilt.

Apply an optimal learning model

I rely on what I call an Optimal Learning Model (OLM; Routman, 2003) for all my teaching and assessing. This model evolved over many years, from a gradual release of responsibility model developed by many scholars—beginning with Pearson and Gallagher (1983)—to an Optimal Learning Model focused on learning; that is, What do learners need in order to achieve optimal success? Although a gradual handover of responsibility is part of the OLM, the most important part is knowing what types of—and how much—demonstration, support, and practice are necessary *before* expecting the learner to productively apply what we are teaching.

I often call the model the "I do it–We do it–We do it–You do it" model because learners often need far more shared experiences than we typically provide them. We often move too fast from "I do it" to "You do it." When that happens, both the students and we become frustrated because we do not get the results we want and expect. Reteaching is necessary, we feel exhausted, and we lose the joy that results from "I can do it!" and "We can do it!" experiences. At the same time, we can overdo the support we give students. It's a delicate dance that requires close observation, ongoing assessment, and thoughtful improvisation as we teach. We always want to be asking ourselves, "What does the learner need most, at this time, to become more competent and independent?"

See the OLM chart to notice who's in charge of the learning. I also believe one of the main reasons students struggle as learners is that we do too much for students for too long. For example, in guided reading, we often wind up doing most of the work and keeping students in the group too long, when in this guided practice phase, students are in charge. Here, we are merely checking and doing the necessary affirming, guiding, and teaching so students have the mindset and skills to read on their own as competent readers who consciously self-monitor, self-evaluate, and self-correct. For more on the OLM, see "Do more frontloading," "Do more demonstrations," "Rely on shared writing," "Do more shared reading," "Put the language in their ears," and "Put guided reading in perspective."

Optimal Learning Model

Who's in charge?	Instructional Support
Moving from dependence to independence	
Teacher/Student	Demonstration
Teacher/Student	Shared Demonstration
Gradual handover of responsibility	
Student/Teacher	Guided Practice
Student/Teacher	Independent Practice

Ongoing cycle of continuous assessment
Celebration of learning
Reteaching, as needed

©2012 Regie Routman

Note. Adapted from *Teaching Essentials: Expecting the Most and Getting the Best from Every Learner, K–8* (p. 89), by R. Routman, 2008, Portsmouth, NH: Heinemann. Copyright 2008 by Regie Routman.

Read professionally

In order to make the wisest decisions for our students and staff, we must be knowledgeable and up-to-date on current and reliable research, educational issues, and best practices. Otherwise, we are unable to intelligently question publishers' resources and district mandates, teach at the highest levels, and effectively advocate for our students and ourselves. Reading professionally is a hallmark of an excellent educator. We may know a lot, but we are always seeking to learn more and do better. Even if we are new to the profession, making professional reading a priority is essential. Ultimately, our deeper knowledge saves us time as we no longer follow programs verbatim and have the know-how to use them as helpful resources.

Take action

- **See if someone in our school or district will serve as a "knowledge sifter"**; that is, a highly informed educator who reads avidly and is willing to sift through the "best" and most relevant research and practices from educational journals and publications, such as *The Reading Teacher*, *Language Arts*, *Voices From the Middle*, *Educational Leadership*, *Phi Delta Kappan*, and *Education Week*—to name a few—and to share those with colleagues.

- **Subscribe to a professional journal**, or share one subscription with one or more colleagues. Whereas reading a professional book can be time consuming, reading an article or two a month is doable.

- **Engage in schoolwide, professional conversations** around professional articles or a book study. A well-informed staff can then intelligently ask, "What does this mean for our literacy practices?" "What might we think about trying or changing?" "What else do we need to know?" and "What are our next steps?"

Plan with the end in mind

The hardest, most intensive, and time-consuming part of my residency work is the planning and deep thinking that take place weeks before we begin the actual demonstration teaching and coaching in classrooms. If we can get the planning "right," in general, the week successfully unfolds. The host classroom teachers and I plan with the end in mind for both students and staff; that is, our driving question is, "What do we want students and teachers to experience, think about, know, and begin to apply by the end of the week?" Planning with the end in mind requires that we do the following:

- ◆ Examine the most pressing literacy issues through a careful look at data, standards, and required curriculum
- ◆ Know and apply proven research and best practices
- ◆ Respect teachers' and students' backgrounds, needs, and interests
- ◆ Engage students' hearts and minds
- ◆ Promote guided discovery and inquiry
- ◆ Remain flexible and open to a change of plans
- ◆ Consider instructional alternatives

While I always have detailed, written teaching plans for the first day and specific, yet general plans for the rest of the week, at the end of each day the host teacher and I sit down to assess how the lesson went, and we discuss and determine the most important next steps for Day 2. We cannot effectively plan for the following day until we have unpacked and evaluated the teaching and learning from the current day.

In a recent residency focused on improving writing instruction, it became clear when planning ahead with the teacher (in whose classroom I would be demonstrating and coaching) that although writing was our focus, student behavior issues were at the top of her list of concerns as well as her colleagues'. On the first day of the residency, after spending some time introducing myself to the students and sharing my life as a reader and writer, I said something like the following to them: "I understand that inappropriate behaviors are a big problem in your classroom, so much so that they interfere with your teacher doing her job and they prevent many of you from learning. So take a few minutes, and turn and talk to the person next to you about the problems this class is having that interfere with learning." Those problems and the solutions we came up with together became a major emphasis for our writing work. Also, by focusing on students first, while knowing the standards and keeping them in mind, we had gone beyond teaching for standards. We were able to teach students—and observing teachers—almost everything about effective writing that we had set out as important end goals for the week:

- Writing for an audience and purpose that matters
- Providing choice, within an agreed-upon structure
- Having the writing form, informational charts with explanations, match the purpose
- Choosing our language carefully
- Rereading and revising to make the message clearer and more concise
- Editing for perfect spelling and conventions to provide a seamless read
- Taking writing well seriously
- Enjoying writing
- Self-evaluating writing effectiveness

Do more demonstrations

Demonstrate everything we want students to be able to do well, from rereading when meaning breaks down to changing classes in an orderly fashion. Keep in mind that one demonstration is rarely sufficient. In fact, in a first demonstration, especially if it's something complex, we tend to pay attention to the procedural parts—steps to follow, details to include. We may not yet know what our questions are. Multiple demonstrations allow us as learners to get a gist of how the parts fit within a meaningful whole. For example, every time I push myself to learn a new technology, at the start, I am only able to go step by step, in sequence, without any real understanding of how these steps fit together. It's only when I've seen multiple demonstrations, including shared experiences where I try out with constant support how to "do it," that I can begin to ask intelligent questions and gain confidence that competence will eventually come.

Take action

- **Explain exactly what will be demonstrated and why**. Check to be sure students understand the purpose. The demonstration might be done by us teachers or it could be done by another expert—even a student, an author through his or her book, a video, or examination of exemplars of student work or other documents where we point out important characteristics and qualities that make the work effective.

- **Think aloud as we read, write, create, and problem solve** so students "see" our in-the-head thinking. Say something like, "I will be thinking out loud, so I can show you exactly what goes on in the mind of a good reader, writer, thinker. Then, I want you to do the same kind of thinking when you read...so you can become an expert reader."

- **Be explicit**. Model exactly what it is we expect students to do. Chart, through a shared writing, what students noticed and saw us do in the demonstration. Use that chart as both an assessment and a rubric.

- **Take charge and be efficient**. Demonstrate for about 10–15 minutes only so students have time and energy left to "try and apply" the work. Demonstrations can be continued the next day. Remember, this is our time to model and explain, so do not get distracted by students who want to offer suggestions. Let them know they will soon have an opportunity to have a turn.

- **Be authentic**. If we expect our students to write on the spot, think about doing our demonstration writing in front of students (instead of showing them a perfect copy we did at home) so they observe our struggles and see writing as a recursive process where we revise, reread, and rethink as we go.

Bond with our students and colleagues

It's difficult to learn from someone we don't trust. Years ago, esteemed New Zealand educator Don Holdaway noted, "You don't have to love every student, but you do need to bond with each one of them if they're to learn anything at all." Bonding means forming meaningful and respectful connections with all students and their families—and making an effort to do the same with our colleagues. I'll never forget seeing the blockbuster movie *Avatar* and being struck that the word *love* was not in the Avatar culture. To express that emotion, a character would say, "I see you" which translated to "I know who you are," "I understand you," "I value you." Too many of our students—and colleagues, too—remain invisible to us. They are physically present but mostly silent. Attempt to "see" through new eyes all members of our school community.

Take action

- **Let every parent or guardian know something positive about the student(s)**. A phone call or note early on—and often, throughout the school year—serves to build trust and saves time in the long run. A parent who believes his or her child is valued will be more likely to listen without feeling threatened and to cooperate when there is a problem. Bonding with families makes it easier to bond with our students.

- **Value students' cultures, interests, and experiences**. The high interest level of a relevant text or curriculum unit, with appropriate support, can make challenging work doable.

- **Share favorite books**, carefully selected to engage students, pique their curiosity and interests, and jump-start conversations where all can join in.

- **Tell personal stories**. Ordinary stories from our lives supplemented with photos of family, friends, and our special interests connect us with students and staff.

- **Choose our language carefully**. The words we use have the power to encourage and motivate or to turn off students—and teachers—from even attempting a task.

- **Celebrate strengths** of teachers, students, administrators, office staff, and community members.

Instill determination to learn

I asked a physician, who spent years of study mastering an extraordinarily difficult procedure, why he was willing to take on such an intricate surgery when only several other peers, nationally and internationally, had been willing to do so. He replied, "It requires determination to learn. There's a long and steep learning curve, but once you learn the technique, it's easy and the results are superior." Having reached a stage of automaticity, where doing the work is mostly second nature, he is able to make the wise, on-the-spot decisions that arise in complex situations that don't fit the norm. By knowing the routines and standard practices thoroughly—through ongoing research and data collection, years of experience, continual learning, and seeking to do better—he can make the inevitable tough judgment calls and expertly adjust his actions with reasonable assurance of an excellent outcome.

It's not much different for us educators. After years of work in diverse schools and classrooms, a crucial learning question persists: Why do teachers, students, and principals in some schools succeed in raising and sustaining achievement for our undeserved students, while so many do not? It often seems to come down to a determination to learn—that is, a steadfast, unwavering commitment to getting better and learning more—no matter what it takes. Having such determination means recognizing where we need to improve, not accepting the status quo, and becoming professionally knowledgeable and highly skilled at our craft. Without that intense, lifelong determination, we simply cannot make a critical and lasting difference for our students.

For our students, instilling a determination to learn is as vital as any literacy or content skills we teach them on their way to becoming self-determining learners. It may, in fact, be the greatest gift we can give them. Instead of giving up when a task or lesson gets frustrating and difficult, we demonstrate how to attain the necessary know-how and persistence that makes eventual success likely. We provide effective and timely instruction, guided practice, and useful feedback so students learn that hard-fought efforts lead to gratification, deep learning, and growing confidence.

For us educators, let us exemplify lifelong determination as learners, the courage to keep on learning in spite of tough political times, and enjoyment with colleagues and students in our lifelong learning process.

Provide more choice within structure

For many of us, we feel that if we give up any control, chaos will result. I like as much order and control as the next person, but here's what I've learned: We get far greater results—not to mention better engagement, enjoyment, and higher quality of work—when students have some choice in what they do. We are still in charge and have the final say, but together we set up expectations and parameters that adhere to curriculum guidelines, standards, and mandates and, at the same time, consider students' background, interests, and needs.

Choice within structure also means that once we've taught students how to do something and they have demonstrated their competence, that activity can become a "free choice" one. For example, students could choose to write poems, book reviews, or persuasive essays when they have completed required work satisfactorily or at designated times when free choice is an option.

Take action

- **Structure assignments within a required framework, but within that framework, give students choice**. For example, we might assign students to write a letter of gratitude to someone who has never been properly thanked for his or her actions. Every student would be expected to follow a writing rubric we create with specific requirements for the letter, but within those requirements, each student would decide to whom they would write and the personal content.

- **Create a bulletin board of choice-within-structure activities**. In a kindergarten classroom, we have a writing wall. Every time we teach a new writing form or genre, we name it and post it on the wall with one or more student exemplars. Students consult the wall daily for ideas. Not only that, the postings serve as a reminder of what has been accomplished throughout the year, and students stop saying to us, "I finished my work. What do I do now?"

- **Give students some say in how activities will be carried out** once they know and apply classroom routines and expectations, for example, choosing places to sit during self-selected reading time, selecting a facilitator and scribe for small-group work, or suggesting a different format for an assignment.

- **Have exemplars available for students, as resources**. Save student work samples from this year's class to share with future students.

Aim to develop self-determining learners

It is not enough that students can complete a task on their own. Just because we can do something independently, such as correctly completing a worksheet or following explicit directions in a guide, doesn't mean we are on our way to becoming lifelong, independent learners. I much prefer aiming for self-determining learners. A self-determining learner sets his own worthwhile goals; continually works on getting better at something that is important; self-monitors his literacy behaviors, attitudes, and actions; set purposes beyond his own self-interest; and self-directs his own learning. Daniel Pink, in his fascinating book *Drive: The Surprising Truth About What Motivates Us*, has written about the three essential elements of self-determination theory: autonomy, mastery, and purpose.

Take action

- **Strive for excellence as a goal**. In conducting reading and writing conferences, impart the message and mind-set that being excellent at something means we are always seeking to improve our abilities.
- **Make sure students "hold then pen" when conferring with them**, and make any necessary adjustments, with our guidance.
- **Ask more questions that make students think for themselves**, such as the following:
  - "Why do you think that?"
  - "I'm not sure I know what you mean. Say more about that."
  - "What else might be the reason for...?"
- **Give students the message that we value and reward their thinking**, backed up by evidence, over a "right" answer that we teachers hold in our heads. We can say something like, "I'm not just interested in a correct answer. If you give me your best thinking and back it up, you can't be wrong."

◆ **Refrain from immediately giving students "the answer."** It's OK to say, "I'm not going to tell you the answer. You can figure this out. We'll come back to this again later after you've had more time to think about it." Or, "Let's figure this out together."

◆ **Provide resources** that encourage and support students to seek "answers"— books, texts, websites, peers, and adults.

Teach rereading

Rereading is one of my most important habits and strategies for being and becoming a more proficient reader, writer, and thinker. I reread favorite books and articles, drafts in process, text passages that are difficult, letters from friends. I reread for sheer pleasure, for fine-tuning of information, to glean deeper meaning, to improve my writing, to savor masterful language and craft, to learn more, to revalue a written piece. Rereading is a powerhouse strategy for increasing fluency, clarity, engagement, enjoyment, and comprehension and, yet, it has been undervalued as a reading and writing tool. We need to demonstrate rereading and show its potential use, guide students in practicing it, and ensure our students apply rereading to their reading and writing repertoires. Not only that, but rereading promotes the close, scrutinized reading that the latest high standards call for. Careful rereading forces us to slow down and think more deeply.

Take action

♦ **Encourage rereading of familiar and favorite texts**. Rereading a well-loved book is like spending time with a treasured friend, an activity that brings us peace and contentment. For learners who struggle, rereading a well-known text makes it easier to practice and achieve fluency, stamina, and greater comprehension.

  • Use class-authored texts from shared writing as familiar texts to reread in the classroom and send home for additional practice.

  • Use partner reading of natural language texts to lead to improved reading competency, which is helpful especially for students who struggle and second-language learners.

  • Use Readers Theatre to create texts from familiar stories to perform for peers. Doing Readers Theatre well requires multiple rereadings.

♦ **Demonstrate rereading as a crucial part of the reading process**. Our readers who struggle are superficial readers. They do not reread when meaning is unclear or words and concepts are unknown. Mostly, they read on whether or not they understand the text.

- **Demonstrate rereading as a crucial part of the writing process**. When demonstrating for students, show the recursive, back and forth nature of composing; that is, in the act of writing, we reread to figure out what to say next, to see if what we've written makes sense, to clarify our thinking, be picky about word choice, improve organization, and so on. I reread my writing-in-process before beginning my writing work each day. We want students to inculcate that same writing habit.

- **Allow a time lapse before revising a draft**. Writers of all ages do a better job on revision when there is a short interim between the writing and final revising; for example, revisiting writing that's done in the morning that afternoon or the following day.

- **Reread to notice what authors do**, including student authors. Notice leads, description, structure and organization, character development, clarity of information, transitions, and much more. Encourage students to apply what authors do as they write. Also, reread students' work to figure out what they are trying to say (see "Embrace public writing conferences," p. 78).

- **Reread aloud to hear the rhythm of the writing**. This strategy is an easy trick of the trade. Reading aloud lets us hear how the piece flows, the rhythm and sounds of the language, and what words may be missing or need to be replaced. I read aloud much of my work in the process of writing and after I write. Reading aloud is especially important for reading and writing poetry.

Share our best ideas

Many years ago, I remember being stingy about sharing my good ideas. I wanted credit for them and was not willing to give them away "for free." A conversation with notable Canadian educator and writer Frank Smith changed my behavior: "Share your ideas with interested colleagues. Where those ideas came from, there are plenty more and they will keep on coming." Generously sharing with colleagues, even if they do not immediately reciprocate, is the mark of a professional who sees the value of all group members of succeeding.

Take action

- **Share** favorite websites, videos, educational blogs, resources, and teaching tips. Start a "Best Ideas" board in the faculty lounge or staff room, and encourage peers to post ideas.

- **Post on social media sites** ideas, strategies, photos, and more. My Facebook page includes photos with captions and information from recent residencies so viewers can "see" effective literacy practices.

- **Offer to demonstrate a lesson**, coteach, or coach in a colleague's classroom. The colleague need not be at the same grade level.

- **Make copies available** of a lesson plan, student work, or an activity that has been very successful, and leave them in the teachers' lounge for interested colleagues.

- **Give credit**. Of course, when we are sharing a colleague's original work, it is important that the author's name is on it, so we recognize the creative source and appropriately credit it in any use or adaptation.

Put guided reading in perspective

A friend and superb teacher of guided reading groups in the intermediate grades came to me, distraught. How was it that her students' reading test scores were lower than her grade-level colleague's? My friend's guided reading lessons were the best I'd ever observed, and she diligently saw four groups every day. Her colleague began each day with a 45-minute, carefully monitored independent reading program where students read "just right," self-selected books connected to a well-organized classroom library. During that time, the colleague conducted in-depth, daily one-on-one reading conferences with students. She did have guided reading groups, but not with every group, every day. My friend's guided reading groups took so long that she often skipped sustained independent reading practice. That's where the critical difference in reading success lies. Without extended practice time, students will not become readers—or writers—regardless of how expertly we conduct our guided reading groups or demonstrations.

In guided reading, the student is in charge and doing most of the reading work. The teacher is checking to ensure the student can read the guided reading group text with at least 95–98% accuracy and with fluency so he can focus on comprehension. The teacher's role is "guide on the side"—nudging, scaffolding, prompting, encouraging, and explicitly teaching as necessary—so that when the student is reading on his own, which is well over 90% of the time, he knows how and when to problem solve, self-monitor, self-question and reread, figure out vocabulary, determine the most important ideas, and so on. It is during the crucial, sustained independent reading time that our students practice, apply, learn, and extend what we have been teaching them. The same principles hold true for writing.

Take action

- ◆ **Increase the amount of opportunities and time students have to respond and participate in productive conversations** about the texts they are reading.
- ◆ **Ensure that carefully monitored, sustained reading practice time is a daily priority.** Too often, sustained reading time is the first activity to go in the language arts block when we run out of time. Consider scheduling that precious reading time first.

- **Reexamine management practices during guided reading**. Be sure that the management—what the other students are doing while we're with groups—is not the main emphasis, overtaking our planning and teaching time as well as our reading priorities.

- **Assess the learning**. Whatever activity our students are doing while we're with a group, we must have a way to evaluate their learning. It is not enough that students are working on-task; we must know if and what they are learning.

- **Consider having students write down their response(s) to a comprehension question**. Ask vital questions (see p. 12) such as "How was the problem solved?" or "What's the most important thing we've learned so far about...?" Using small notebooks for this purpose works well. Having students record their responses is also important when we assign further reading, because once we ask a comprehension question orally in a group and one student responds, we don't know if the others "got it."

Examine our management focus

A teacher approached me with a dilemma; she was trying to "fit in" multiple reading groups a day but admitted that "managing the management" was taking most of her time and energy. This was in kindergarten! Although students must know what to do—and be able to manage that time without our help—while we are working with other students, we must ask ourselves if our management system is taking priority over learning. The more deeply knowledgeable we are about teaching and learning, the more easily our management practices are seamlessly integrated into our instruction. Also, when our lessons are engaging and relevant, students are motivated to stay focused on their task, which minimizes teacher management. Most important, and often ignored, we must be able to assess everything students are doing when they are working on their own. That is, we must know, supported by evidence, that students are learning more, not just keeping quietly busy. Chances are, if we are struggling with management issues, we are also struggling with our teaching. While it's true that effective classroom management must be in place before we can fully focus on instruction, look to put in place meaningful activities that drive learning forward.

Take action

- ◆ **Ensure that the management system is literacy based and curriculum based**, that students are absolutely clear on what they are to do, that they have received enough support to "do it," that the procedures and activities are worth the students' time and efforts, and that we are assessing everything we ask them to do.

- ◆ **Use our small-group work to assign further reading**.

  - Have students reread for a specific purpose. For example, after a guided reading group, have them reread for fluency, to answer an inferential question in writing, or both. During the next meeting time with that group, check students' written responses and instruct, as needed.

  - Have students read on in a text, independently or with a partner, once we are certain students can read and understand the text. Give students a key question and have them answer briefly, in writing, which will show whether they have understood the text.

◆ **Model, explain, and practice the behaviors we expect students to exhibit**. Notice and comment on what students are doing well. Let students know that exemplary behaviors are an expectation. Say something like, "I noticed that Jason's group worked well together. They made sure everyone had a chance to speak, they each made eye contact with the speaker, and they were careful not to interrupt a speaker. That's what I expect from all groups."

◆ **Assess students' self-management**. One sure way to tell if students are assuming responsibility for our expected behaviors is if they carry on, as usual, even when we are not present, such as when there is a substitute teacher.

◆ **Check ourselves**. How much time are we spending to remind students to behave, follow established procedures, and work out behavioral issues? Such time should be minimal.

Seek to do better

I think one of the differences between an ordinary teacher and an extraordinary one may be that the extraordinary teacher is always seeking to improve and, in fact, has the conviction that it is almost always possible to do a better job. I believe as well, that one of our major problems as a society is that we lack the collective and indomitable will to dramatically improve education for our most underserved students. We settle for far too little because we do not collectively believe that all students can learn at high levels.

In that regard, the book *Better: A Surgeon's Notes on Performance* by Atul Gawande (2007) has greatly influenced me. Gawande is a brilliant and humble surgeon who writes about what it takes for doctors to do better to treat patients more successfully and to cure diseases that have been resistant to prescribed treaments; basically, it's a relentless pursuit of excellence and a refusal to accept poor performance. The parallels to teaching and school change are striking. Gawande calls himself a "positive deviant," a term I have happily adopted for a person who strives to make a "worthy difference." Gawande writes,

> Arriving at meaningful solutions is an inevitably slow and difficult process. Nonetheless, what I saw was: better is possible. It does not take genius. It takes diligence. It takes moral clarity. It takes ingenuity. And above all, it takes a willingness to try. (p. 246)

Seeking to follow his own advice, Gawande also writes, in his article in *The New Yorker* entitled "Personal Best," how he approached an eminent surgeon he greatly admired and asked if the surgeon would be willing to coach him. Although Gawande had never before been coached and his reputation is already impeccable, his goal was and is continuous improvement. What he learned surprised and enlightened him. His coach saw small things Gawande had never thought about because he could not see the surgery from the coach's vantage point. The suggestions were small things to tweak the accomplishments of an already excellent practitioner, but the scrupulous attention to nuanced detail added up to an improved result.

For us as educators, Gawande is a role model for being relentless about our own continuous improvement. Getting better requires constant reflection on our own practices, humility, willingness to embrace coaching opportunities, and a readiness to do whatever it takes to become as masterful as possible at our craft.

Become an active listener

Most of us who teach talk a lot. It's been well documented that, for the most part, we talk much more than our students do. Some of us have strong opinions that we freely disperse, and sometimes we can come across as a bit bossy. Certainly, these factors have been true for me. I know I need to work on becoming a better listener rather than listening politely before I can speak again. That is, we need to listen with nothing more in mind than, "What is this person trying to say?" That nonjudgmental mind-set and single-minded concentration are crucial for successful conferring in writing, for understanding our peers' point of view, for making every member of the school community feel valued, and for hearing all the voices (see "Promote more opportunities for speaking," p. 160).

Take action

- **Increase the amount of time and opportunity we give students to participate in focused discussions**. Provide more "turn and talk" time with a partner as well as more small-group collaboration, both guided and self-directed.

- **Do not repeat what a student says**. When we do so, we give the message that other students need not listen to anyone except us teachers. We not only stifle students' voices, but also we inadvertently encourage students to ignore what their peers are saying.

  - Say something like, "I'm not going to repeat what Mario says, so, Mario, you need to speak loudly so your classmates can hear you. And, students, you need to pay close attention to what Mario says."

  - Have students "turn and talk" with a partner. Ask, "What did Mario just say?" Call on anyone. If a student cannot respond, ask his partner to tell him what Mario said, and then have the first student either put those thoughts in his own words or repeat what his partner just said.

  - Have Mario repeat what he said if both students in the pair cannot respond. Then repeat the entire exercise until students can respond.

- **Let students know we will only give directions once**. If students know from our past behaviors that we will restate what they are to do, there's no reason for them to listen the first time.

- **Establish and practice listening guidelines with students** such as making eye contact with the speaker, not interrupting, and demonstrating respectful posture, such as sitting up tall.

- **Expect all students working together, with a partner or in a small group, to be able to state the groups' findings**. Say something like, "It's important for you to listen to each other. At the end of group time, I should be able to call on your partner or any group member to say what you learned, decided, questioned, concluded, and so on."

- **Listen to the quality of discourse** between students as they talk with each other. Are the questions and comments of quality and significance? We need to remember to model effective discourse and questioning techniques throughout the day.

Reward persistence

Students, as well as we educators, need to believe and value that a steadfast effort leads to success and that failure is inherent—and even necessary—in order to achieve a worthy goal. My greatest learning has come from lessons that don't go well. Then I am forced to examine and analyze what went wrong and to ask myself, "What *didn't* I do to make it possible for students to succeed?" "What do I need to do now?" Usually, it's that I haven't been clear enough or provided enough background, demonstrations, and shared experiences before students tried to apply the new learning. So we begin again. With renewed effort, success eventually comes.

Research has repeatedly shown that rewarding performance can have possible negative consequences and work against collaboration and intrinsic motivation. But rewarding persistence and hard work with specific, timely, and honest feedback sends the message that we value effort and that it is sustained effort that leads to lasting learning and success, not just smartness. Not only that, but research by Carol Dweck (2007) showed that students who were told their success was due to their hard work were much more likely to challenge themselves as learners and to take more risks than those who were told their success was due to being smart.

Making an effort has to be taught. Students who are used to praise and rewards for performance, as well as those used to negative comments for not measuring up, need to experience—with our guidance and support—the internal satisfaction and reward that come from making a full-out effort.

Take action

- **Give credit to students' problem solving and thinking processes** as well as to the final product or "right answer." Be sure to value effort and responses in whole-class discussion, one-on-one conferences, small-group work, and homework in determining a student's grade.
- **Value group thinking**. When students collaborate in small groups, require a joint written response that shows evidence of their collaborative thinking and explanations, for example, the various solutions they attempted in figuring out a math problem.

- **Share stories of challenging experiences where making a hard-fought effort eventually led to success**. Begin by sharing a personal story. Then encourage similar story telling with a partner and within small group. Also, read and discuss stories of adversity where unrelenting effort led to success. (For examples, see *Teaching Essentials* website www.regieroutman.com/teachingessentials/default.asp. Click "Text Resources" and "I Can Do It! A Selected Book List to Inspire Hope.")

- **Give the message that we greatly value earnest effort**, and that we will do all we can to support and foster students and colleagues who demonstrate determination to learn. Seek to make working hard and persistence a highly valued part of our classroom and school culture.

Focus on the writer first and the writing second

Of everything we do to help turn students into writers, focusing first on the writer and trying to discern what the writer is trying to say is the most crucial. It is one of the hardest things to accomplish as a teacher of writing because it depends on us adopting a mind-set of noticing and celebrating student strengths, first and foremost. Focusing on the writer first also requires us to be thinking, "When the student leaves the conference, I want him to have the confidence, energy and will to go on writing." Therefore, the language we use with each student must be carefully chosen to celebrate that student's strengths and to build upon those strengths. This can be difficult for us as teachers because we sincerely want improvement as quickly as possible. We tend to be skimpy with honest compliments. Keep this in mind: The language we use with a student in a writing conference has the power to change that student's life. Time and time again, I have seen a struggling student sit up taller, finally make eye contact, smile, gain respect from his peers, begin to take risks and blossom into a full-fledged writer—all because the student has been celebrated for his writing efforts and what he is trying to say. Conversely, we can demolish a student's writing spirit for the whole school year by focusing first on weaknesses and strategies for improvement.

Take action

- **Encourage the student to read his paper aloud** during a writing conference. Just listen for the whole of what the student is trying to say. Try not to look at the writing itself. In that way, we are not distracted by poor handwriting, spelling, and a messy paper and can truly focus on the content and intended message of the writer.

- **Pay particular attention to the language the writer is using**—or attempting to use—and how that language has an impact on a reader before worrying about structure, conventions, grammar, and so forth.

- **Focus on the student's strengths**. Be thinking: "What is this student trying to accomplish? What has he done well or tried to do? How can I best recognize and support his efforts?"

- **Choose and use language that moves the writer forward**. Be thinking: "What's the most important thing I can say or do right now that will give the writer the will and energy to go on writing?"
- **Notice the student's body language and affect**. Students let us know, without speaking, how they view themselves as writers. Be sensitive to the signals they send us, and do whatever we can to boost the writer's competence and confidence.

Expect more

I recently spent a day in a school where 80% of the students qualified for free and reduced-cost meals, and almost all were English-language learners. Achievement at the school had been dismal for years. The talented principal, who was bilingual and bicultural, had grown up in this community, was one of the few in her high school to attend and graduate college, and had returned with a steadfast commitment to increase possibilities for her underserved Hispanic students. After proudly giving me a tour around the school, where teaching and learning were now vibrant in every classroom, she was eager for me to meet the superintendent and assistant superintendent. In our conversation with them, I asked, "How many of the students in your district go on to college?" Without missing a beat, they answered, "Our students don't go on to college." Neither administrator could cite any numbers because they collected no such data; they simply didn't believe or expect that their students could be college material. My principal colleague and I were stunned and heartbroken but not really surprised.

In far too many schools, we make excuses and accept stagnant or low achievement and play a blame game. We use poverty and other outside factors to shirk our responsibility, maintain our low expectations, and to fail to acknowledge that we can do better. While it is true that we cannot compensate for the myriad of complex issues many of our students come to school with, we can and must give them our finest efforts for the hours they are with us each day. We need to raise our expectations for what's possible, see our students as capable and resilient, and assume responsibility for the achievement of *all* students. In my 40 plus years of teaching and coaching in schools, it is low expectations on the part of adults in the school that most impede optimal student learning. Those diminished expectations often lead to a watered down curriculum, low-level language use, skills taught in isolation, and scripted programs that isolate students from potentially rich and authentic literacy and language experiences.

However, with higher expectations and excellent, targeted teaching, we can raise achievement and change lives (see "Seek to do better," p. 33). For an example of a former special education student and nonreader who has gone on to a college with aspirations to become a lawyer, click "View Success Story" at www.regieroutman.com/inresidence/overview.aspx for the student's own words.

Read aloud every day

Every time I work in a school, I bring books as gifts for the school and classrooms. I choose those books carefully, often with the help of a librarian or children's book specialist at my local, independent bookstore. Often I choose a book above many students' reading level but at their listening level, which is usually higher. I want to stimulate their nonfiction interests, increase their awareness about important issues, and have them savor a beautifully written story. If students are to become proficient readers and writers, they need to hear the rich language of literature, notice author's craft, and relish how a talented author uses words, format, illustrations, and more. Do not give up reading aloud! It's a peaceful, pleasurable activity for our students and us, and it's an opportunity to introduce various genres, learn about authors, expand vocabulary, and provide inspiring role models for writing.

Take action

- ◆ **Connect reading with writing**. Guide and encourage readers to notice what authors do, including student authors, and to try some of those things out in their own writing.

- ◆ **Make students aware of the way authors choose and use language when reading aloud**.

  - • Stop occasionally and reread something an author has done well. Say something like, "I just have to read this part again. Listen to how the author's lead (beginning) hooks the reader right away. I can't wait to read on. Take a look at the lead in your story and make sure you pull your readers in."

  - • Or before independent reading time, we might say, "Today, when you're reading on your own, pay special attention to a place where the author describes a setting (or character or event) so you can picture it. You may want to attempt something similar in your own writing." Once in a while, have them mark that place with a sticky note and then take time to have students read some of those passages aloud—to the class, in a small group, or with a partner.

◆ **Promote reading aloud by families, regardless of students' ages**. Many parents tend to stop reading aloud once children can read on their own, but reading to older children creates a strong family bond and can introduce them to the wonder of language in all types of texts and genres.

◆ **Vary read-aloud texts**. Create routine opportunities to read magazine articles, news stories, book reviews, travel articles, and exemplary student work.

◆ **Read aloud often**—more than once a day, if possible. It's also a wonderful way to bring the day to a peaceful close.

Treat all members of the school community respectfully

I'll never forget reading about a prominent CEO who said he never hired an employee for a key position without seeing how the prospective job seeker treated people at his present job. In particular, the CEO watched to see how and if the job seeker knew and interacted with secretarial and custodial staff and those not in leadership positions. The CEO never hired anyone who didn't treat all employees as team members. It's an important message to take to heart.

Take action

- **Ensure that a welcoming message to families is highly visible** as soon as visitors enter the school building. It can be daunting for families whose children have mostly known failure to even enter our schools and classrooms.

- **Get to know students, teachers, and community members**, and greet them by name.

- **Treat secretaries and custodians as key players in a school's success**. Use Thanksgiving, Valentine's Day, and other holidays to write class-authored gratitude letters. Invite them into the classroom to talk about their jobs. Proudly include them in any whole-school activity that celebrates the school's achievement.

- **Invite all staff members to attend professional development meetings**. Include specialists and teaching aides. Consider inviting a parent, too.

- **Resist judging families, even when they fail to "show up."** We never know how many hardships a family may be facing or what fears or negative past experiences may be keeping them from attending a conference or returning a phone call. Continue to reach out in a positive manner.

Connect writing with reading

Without exception, I begin every teaching residency with the reading–writing connection. I share my reading and writing life and explain how I could not be a writer if I were not a discerning reader. As well, I read aloud to students an outstanding book or two that I have brought the class and we notice what authors do and carry this into our writing. Reading enhances writing, and writing can improve our reading abilities. Yet this powerful connection is often overlooked and undervalued and, most often, reading and writing are artificially separated. While the latest standards do not directly connect reading and writing, they do specify an integrated model of literacy: "The processes of communication are closely connected, as reflected throughout this document" (National Governors Association Center for Best Practices & Council of Chief State School Officers, 2010, p. 4).

Take action

- **Use exemplary texts and authors to demonstrate what authors do**. Include student-authored texts. With our guidance, have students continuously notice literary language, logical organization, engaging leads, satisfying closings, descriptive settings, effective transitions, and so on.

- **Teach students to read like writers**. Occasionally, direct them to read for a literary or informational device, such as an unusual, riveting lead or the use of visuals and organizational structure that provide additional information and text access.

- **Make available and accessible outstanding texts in various genres**. Include picture books for younger and older readers.

- **Do more poetry reading and writing**. Poetry is a terrific genre for equalizing writing achievement and having all students excel. Immerse students in free verse poetry, notice and chart what poets do, and write some poems together before students write their own. Put together with students a classroom poetry anthology, and make a second edition as a model for future classes.

- **Write more book reviews**, not book reports (which only exist in schools).

- **Use daily writing to teach reading to learners who struggle**. Students' own language and stories often become their most successful and enjoyable reading experiences, which can jump-start the entire reading process. Explicit word work can easily be taught in the context of these texts (see p. 51).

(see p. 51)

- ◆ **Make the reading–writing connection seamless**. Beginning in the primary grades, support students' writing with excellent reading texts. For example, if students are writing about planets, sharks, or plants, bring in texts they can read to provide evidence, facts, and ideas to support and enrich their writing.

- ◆ **Save copies of student-authored books** from previous years to supplement reading texts early in the new school year.

See *Transforming Our Teaching Through Reading/Writing Connections* (Routman, 2008c) to view the reading/writing connection in daily classroom practice.

Celebrate learners' strengths

One of the most dramatic and significant changes I've made in my teaching and coaching is to notice and celebrate everything the learner has done well. When we celebrate the learner, we make honest statements that explicitly acknowledge and name learner's accomplishments. A celebration in writing might be as small as dating the paper or as big as taking initiative to reread a draft and then rewrite a better lead. My training as a Reading Recovery Teacher decades ago helped me make a permanent mind shift from focusing first on a student's needs to noticing and acknowledging strengths. If the child in Reading Recovery knew only the first letter of his first name, his evaluation noted that fact first, and that's where the teaching began—building on that child's strength(s). Discarding a deficit mentality is difficult. Many years ago, when visiting schools in New Zealand, I bought a bag of potato chips. "Please dispose of this thoughtfully" was written on the back. I was taken aback by that positive language and looked for just the right place to discard the bag! What a difference affirmative language makes in the actions we take. In the United States, our typical message would be "Don't litter." Celebration does indeed have the power to change not just actions, but also students' and teachers' lives.

Take action

- **Focus first on everything the learner is doing well and attempting to do** when conferring or coaching in reading or writing. Name those strengths, write them down, and read them back. Eventually, with practice and guidance, have the learner list and name his or her strengths and then we only state what has been left out. Noticing a learner's strengths before moving to suggestions is as necessary for teachers as it is for students.

- **Give at least several honest compliments before making a suggestion**. Research has shown that most of us need to hear at least six positive comments before being open to constructive criticism.

- **Name the exact, unique language a learner has used in writing, coaching, speaking, or evaluating**. In that way, we are providing a model for other learners and can say something like, "Notice how Anna phrased that question. You might want to try it that way too, in your writing or speaking."

- **See all adults in the school community as learners**—teachers, principals, coaches, superintendents, district administrators, parents, and so on.

Be a reader

Several years ago, while speaking at a K–12 literacy conference of about 500 educators, I asked, "How many of you have read *Olive Kitteridge* by Elizabeth Strout?" The book had just won the Pulitzer Prize for literature, and I had found the beautifully written story of a troubled, retired schoolteacher to be profoundly moving. I wanted to connect with the audience and see how many others had read and savored the book too. Just a few hands went up, and I confess I was shocked. The meager response led me to ask that question again, at other conferences, and the results were always the same. We who teach reading are not always readers! Quite simply, we cannot be expert teachers of reading, across the curriculum, without being readers ourselves.

Letting our colleagues and students know we are readers and sharing our reading lives with them are essential for turning them on to wide reading for pleasure and information. See my blog posts at www.regieroutman.org for books I've read over a six-month period. I post the books I've read since the last posting and discuss one or more favorites. In those postings, I have also shared commentaries on my reading habits—which I use to inform and guide my teaching—such as keeping a reading log, belonging to a monthly book club, preparing for a book discussion, rereading favorite books, reading more nonfiction, knowing what I'm going to read next, keeping a stack of books by my bedside table, reading magazines and journal articles, and much more. I share all of these when I go into classrooms, and, as previously noted, I always bring some favorite books with me to pique students' and teachers' interests.

Implement standards thoughtfully

So many of us are hopeful about the latest standards, the Common Core State Standards (CCSS). They set a necessary, higher bar for what students should know and be able to do, especially as related to analytical thinking in reading and writing texts and in content knowledge. Left to states to set the literacy bar, far too many lowered standards and expectations in order to artificially raise student achievement. As a result, falsely elevated test scores on high-stakes tests did a terrible disservice to many students and their families who came to believe students were progressing satisfactorily when they were not. Compared with scores on the National Assessment of Educational Progress in many states, the differences in achievement between the state test and the national test were stark.

Still, while the new standards have much to offer us, there are cautions. Standards are likely, at least at first, to raise expectations but fragment instruction. Just like focusing on an extensive checklist, it's easy to lose sight of the students in front of us for the checklist or standard and to discard what we know works from research and experience. Very troublesome is the proliferation of commercial materials being labeled and created as implementation cure-alls, Also, as publishers explicitly connect standards to new and costly tests, we're likely to further escalate our national frenzy of test more, teach less.

There is only one implementation route that will enable us to truly raise and sustain literacy achievement and that is a whole-school commitment to intelligent and effective professional development. Such a commitment requires a national, cultural shift that recognizes that only highly knowledgeable educators can read and interpret standards—which delineate the "what" of teaching, the performance expectations, to effectively determine the "how" of teaching, the instructional and assessment moves that lead to student competency. Knowing and applying "best" literacy practices that respect the long-standing research base on literacy acquisition and application and holding fast to making trustworthy decisions that honor our students' backgrounds, interests, and needs are essential to implementing standards with instructional integrity.

What follows are a few broad and significant areas we can focus on that are cited in the CCSS as necessary for college and career readiness. Note that these key areas are trademarks of highly effective and knowledgeable teaching regardless of what set of standards happen to be in place at the time.

- **Critical thinking**

  Focus on in-depth learning—not just right answers—requiring more analysis and real-world problem solving. Critical thinking includes teaching independent thinking; that is, reasoning abstractly, constructing persuasive arguments, understanding point of view, and asking questions that cause deeper thinking, such as "What made you think that?" "What's another possibility?" "How else might this information be interpreted?" (see "Ask more vital questions," p. 12). A caution here is not to teach critical thinking—or any standard—as a separate entity, but to envision critical thinking infused throughout the day and across the curriculum.

- **Close and deep reading of texts, including more nonfiction**

  Teach students to read more closely and analytically—both informational and literary texts—by going back to a text to cite evidence, a necessary skill for proficient readers. That type of reading, recommended by CCSS, need not be exclusive; that is, we can do close reading of text and still employ our experiences and prior knowledge, which are long established, research-based hallmarks of strong readers (see "Use common sense," p. 124 and "Create access to complex texts," p. 135).

- **Extensive writing across the curriculum**

  Emphasize the teaching of clear and coherent writing in all subject areas and in multiple genres for various audiences and purposes, supported first by effective demonstrations of our own effective thinking and writing. Include persuasive arguments, research, narratives, reflections, explanations, and much more.

Make certain students are engaged, not just on-task

A middle grades teacher, who invited me into her classroom, told me her students were participating in sustained reading of self-selected texts every day, but many of them were not engaged. What should she do? A show of hands confirmed that at least half the class admitted to not enjoying the book they were reading. To an outside observer the impression was "these students are engaged," but silence, making eye contact, and compliant behavior can be deceiving. In some classrooms, silence indicates students have had few opportunities for conversations, or they don't know what their questions are or how to make informed choices, or both. Engaged learners are "hooked"—they are working in their learning zone. They know why and what they are doing, and they possess the skills and learning habits to be successful. They are motivated, value the task at hand, and can discuss its purpose. They can problem solve when meaning breaks down.

Take action

- **Provide more choice within structure**, as previously discussed (p. 23).
- **Make the instruction and learning relevant**. Take the required curriculum and personalize it for students. Make it relevant and content-rich.
- **Move at a steady pace**. Stop while interest is still high.
- **Only talk for about 10 minutes**. Then give students a short "break" through "turn and talk," small-group conversation, or movement so they have time to process and respond to what they've heard.
- **Assess as we go**. Check that students are "getting" what we are teaching. Reteach as needed. It's hard to stay engaged if we don't understand what's going on.

Integrate word study across the curriculum

The only way to "fit everything in," because there are never enough minutes in the day, is to be as efficient as possible. Not only that, but learning is faster and more likely to be long lasting when we can see the value of the work and immediately apply what is being taught. Explicit daily word study, in the context of the literacy or content lesson, is a big shift for some of us, but most teachers quickly see the benefit—faster learning that sticks.

Midyear in a kindergarten classroom, where students were learning about nutrition and their community, each student wrote a restaurant review that got sent to the local restaurant. Using vocabulary and concepts students had learned from our reading aloud of relevant books, examining real-life brochures and menus, and discussing personal experiences, we first wrote a restaurant review together on chart paper. On the first and second reading, we read it through line by line, and on the subsequent reading, we used a sliding mask to highlight high frequency words such as "red" in Red Robin restaurant. The second day, the whole class read a word-processed copy of our class authored review. Then we zeroed in on a few high-frequency words and, word by word, talked about the "tricky part," visually highlighted and studied each word for a few moments ("take a picture in your brain"), and had each child write the designated word on a whiteboard. The restaurant review, which we covered up for each word writing assessment, was then uncovered as we asked students, "Check yourself. Do you have it right? If not, fix it up." Just about every student could write—with some self-correction—the words *red*, *love*, and *food*.

Take action

- **Post word walls in science and social studies for key vocabulary** we expect students to read and write.
- **Use individual whiteboards to have all students quickly write and read featured words**. Include challenge words. In the aforementioned kindergarten restaurant reviews, *pizza* was our challenge word, and almost every student—mid-year in a high needs, half-day kindergarten class—spelled it correctly! They could all read *pizza* too.

- **Expect students to self-check spelling** through using room resources such as charts and word walls, checking with peers, and looking at familiar texts.

- **Create with the students, from the reading and writing we are doing, charts that conform to the word study in process**, for example, a chart of "ee" words or an important vowel combination students must know, or words with specific prefixes or suffixes or important roots. Students can use sticky notes to attach words to the chart and, if they are correctly spelled, add them to the chart.

- **Highlight features of words in familiar texts**—using a document camera or on charts, and so on. Use a sliding mask to feature a word and to blend word parts.

- **Evaluate everything we are teaching in word work.** One quick and reliable way is to take a familiar text, such as a class-authored one (for example, our restaurant review) and give each student a word-processed copy. Read through the text as a whole. Afterwards, direct students to circle designated words, turn their papers over and write those words, and then self-check and correct for accuracy. Send home such papers weekly and have students read the text to their family and talk about the text and their word work learning.

Imagine the possibilities

After a recent workshop, a teacher asked, "How do you teach kids to imagine?" It was a question I'd never heard before, and I was surprised and saddened by it. We live in an age where constant screen time is a way of life and children are often overscheduled, so it isn't all that surprising the question came up. I responded, "You don't really teach kids to imagine. You provide the time, space, and resources, and it will happen." But the question stayed with me: "How do you teach kids to imagine?" A family story shed some light.

After persistent requests from our granddaughters—who were 6 and 9 years old at the time—my husband Frank designed and supervised the construction of a beautiful tree house/tea house, high up on the top of a hill in our back yard. The setting is peaceful, and the views of old growth treetops and glimpses of a nearby lake are lovely. Frank deliberately left the interior of the structure spare, with just a few shelves, a stool and a bench, and a hand-sanded piece of beautiful bark to serve as a table or desk. The girls were thrilled, and the very first question they asked when the tree house was completed was, "Can we bring up the computer?" I told them, "You get to use the computer in your home and ours, too. The tree house is a place for you to have time to imagine." At first the girls were stymied about how to use the space and we could tell they were bored, but little by little, over many months, they began to figure things out. They put favorite books and objects on the shelves, used blank notebooks to write stories, poems, and notes, planted a garden, foraged for wild berries, created trails "through the woods," read books in a rope hammock, picked flowers and arranged them in vases, and much more. Given the time, space, and opportunities—along with providing choice within structure, which we have previously discussed—children do begin to imagine the possibilities.

Observe an excellent kindergarten teacher

Some years ago, our school district got a group of K–12 teachers together to determine a coherent literacy plan across the grades. I still recall the shock of secondary teachers, after several days of cross-grade-level collaboration, as they shifted their views of kindergarten teachers from "cut and paste teachers" to deep respect for "smart and savvy colleagues." They, along with many of us, have no idea how much it takes to be an expert kindergarten teacher. In my 40 plus years of teaching in many diverse schools, kindergarten teachers are often the most knowledgeable. They are usually well grounded in theory, practice, management, pacing, relationships, and the importance of play for learning and socializing. They seamlessly integrate music, drama, movement, and the arts into all they do. While corners such as a vet clinic or grocery store, building with blocks, painting on easels, and dress up have sadly disappeared from many kindergarten classrooms as the push for academics trickles down, determined and wise kindergarten teachers have managed to hold onto sacred play time and to integrate explicit teaching into authentic writing and reading activities throughout the day.

Take action

- **Do everything possible to ensure that the kindergarten teacher(s) in our schools have high enough expectations and get high results**. With expert literacy teaching, almost all students can leave kindergarten as emerging and beginning readers and writers, which, in turn, raises achievement possibilities for the whole school. Noted researcher Richard Allington (2011) states, "Better trained kindergarten teachers can solve the reading problems of at-risk students at the same rate as expert tutorial programs..." (p. 41).
- **Seek out an exemplary kindergarten teacher, and spend time in her or his classroom** even if we teach in an upper grade, middle school, or high school. When we view the teaching process as a continuum and with an open mind, we see connections for our own grade level. More important, the joy is still

there. Kindergartners are full of energy and an "I can do it" spirit, which is a good reminder of how we want all kids to be.

♦ **Advocate for putting more resources into kindergarten** and ensuring that kindergarten teachers are highly proficient, that class size is small, and that all-day kindergarten becomes a reality everywhere. With excellent first teaching for all students, we prevent literacy problems before they occur, increase educational opportunities for more students, and save money in the long run.

Take time to reflect

I recently gave a blank journal as a gift to a principal and to a curriculum director. They laughed when they read the large gold type on the bright red cover, "Keep calm and carry on," a quote by Winston Churchill from the Second World War. Our lives move so quickly in and out of school that it's hard to remember what we did and said just a half hour ago, and it's impossible to make sense of it all on the run. Keep a notebook handy and record thoughts and ideas from anything related to teaching, learning, coaching, leading, or anything that strikes you as important to remember. I use one spiral notebook for all my reflections on daily teaching, professional development, conferences I attend, and things I'm thinking about. I date my entries, reread them, make notes in the margins, and return to them to clarify my thinking and next steps. Keeping everything together in one notebook, which can last me for a couple of years, means I can always find my notes!

Take action

- **Take a few moments between lessons or classes to record our insights**, questions that have arisen, new thinking, confirmations, ideas for future teaching, and so on. If we don't write our thoughts down, we lose them. Let students know why we do this reflective writing. They may want to try out something similar for themselves with their own notebooks.

- **Record exact language used**, which is nonjudgmental, when observing a colleague or teacher, and give those words to the teacher. Teachers can read their own instructional language later on and reflect upon it. In our moment-by-moment teaching, we rarely remember the words we have used, and words matter.

- **Carry a notebook** when leaving the classroom, attending a meeting, and heading home. That allows for "catching" thoughts as they arise and for re-reading for focused reflection, at a later time.

- **Purchase a smaller notebook**, such as a Moleskin, available in various sizes at bookstores and other shops, and carry in a pocket or purse. I love mine and always have it with me. Kids love these too!

- **Take advantage of technical devices**, such as a smartphone, iPad, or e-reader to record thoughts, reflections, and memorable language.

◆ **Consider using our notes to write an editorial, a professional article, or even a book for educators**. Although we may think all the important stories have already been told, it's not true. Our story in our own words is unique and needs to be heard. Truly, one of the major differences between a writer and a nonwriter is a writer writes! I try to heed the wisdom of Donald Murray, Pulitzer prize–winning journalist, teacher and author, who said, "No writing is ever wasted" and "Never a day without a line."

Form unlikely friendships

There's a marvelous nonfiction book, *Unlikely Friendships*, by Jennifer Holland, that I often bring as a gift to a school when I do a teaching residency. The book's subtitle, *47 Remarkable Stories From the Animal Kingdom*, aptly describes the unexpected ways—in compelling text and gorgeous photos—that remarkable friendships bloom and prosper between two very different creatures. Each two- or three-page short story serves as a great read-aloud, model for excellent writing, and captivating tale for all ages. *Unlikely Friendships* books have also been written in smaller, shorter versions for young readers. Also, *Friends: True Stories of Incredible Animal Friendships* by Catherine Thimmesh is another terrific nonfiction picture book that can serve a similar purpose for young readers.

There's another reason I love the book. It is to subtly suggest to teachers and the principal that they rely on each other, even when it feels awkward or strange to do so. As we have already noted, the culture of a school speaks volumes about school-wide achievement. Where there are cliques and gossip and school areas where some members are not welcome, a school cannot and does not thrive, and whole-school student achievement cannot be realized or sustained. For a healthy school community, every member needs to work towards developing trust with all other members.

Take action

- **Sit next to someone we don't normally associate with** at a staff or professional development meeting. Even if we are not comfortable talking to that person yet, our proximity and body language can indicate a neutral or welcoming stance.

- **Approach unlikely mentors—that is, teachers we admire who are not at our grade level**. If the kindergarten teacher has a reputation for being terrific at shared writing—the story telling, pacing, keeping students engaged—make plans to observe him or her even if we teach a fifth-grade class. Recognize that there are genuine teaching insights we can gain from observing any outstanding colleague.

- **Strike up conversations** with peers we don't usually talk to. Take the first, deliberate step to get to know colleagues better. For example, honestly compliment another teacher we might not reach out to every day.

- **Form a partnership or triad from different grade levels** and coach each other, for example, in how to confer with students, which takes lots of practice and feedback to do well.

- **Offer to work with the principal to reconfigure the location of classrooms so the school operates as one unit,** not as a divided community. Or, again, offer to work on the master schedule for maximum flexibility and equity across the grades.

Recognize that all learners have special needs

Most of the teaching I do in my residency work is in schools where the majority of students come from low-income families with high needs. As well, there are large numbers of English-language learners, high student mobility rates, and growing numbers of students who are homeless. I passionately believe that education is the main route to the American dream and that unequal educational opportunity for underserved students is the gravest civil rights issue of our time. I have also learned that all schools are high needs schools in different ways.

Several years ago, in the same district where I was working in a school where most students qualified for subsidized lunches, a respected colleague urged me to do a writing residency in a school where most students were growing up privileged in terms of high financial stability. When she told me the needs at the affluent school were also great, I remained skeptical, but because of my high regard for her, I acquiesced. I was surprised to find that teachers' expectations for students at the affluent school were generally low, as was literacy knowledge for highly effective teaching. Because students' test scores were very high each year, attributed mostly to families' large income and high educational levels, many teachers were complacent with the mediocre work students did in class. At the end of the week, some of the fourth graders thanked me for the "gifted" teaching, which stunned me because the high-level teaching was the same as what I do in all schools.

The focus for the week centered on writing about a dream, a goal or ambition, students have for the future. In the high poverty schools where I have worked, students, given the same topic, typically wrote about wanting to make the world a better place, for example, by becoming a doctor to help the poor or to get a good education in order to buy a house for their family. Here, in the affluent school, students overwhelmingly wrote about wanting to spend more time with their families. What poignantly came through was that while these children had everything money could buy, what they wanted most from their busy and high achieving parents was more time with them. Because this "Dreams" topic was dear to them and their letters were addressed to their parents—through our explicit demonstrations, guidance, and very high expectations—these letters were far better than their usual writing. A big take-away from that residency was that *all* students need and deserve expert, "gifted" teaching, from our most profoundly struggling ones to the most gifted ones and that we must be very knowledgeable, dedicated professionals to give it to them.

Choose and use excellent texts

We can't teach a first-rate reading lesson with a second-rate book, and we can't effectively teach craft in writing without outstanding literature. Neither can we teach well and deeply in the content areas without primary sources and reliable resources that are accurate, well written, and appropriately challenging. While it can be daunting to keep up with the most current and relevant texts that best suit our goals and purposes, we can consult websites, librarians, news media, bookstores, colleagues, and social media for recommendations. Then we can use our read-aloud times, demonstration lessons, whole-class and small-group work, and reading and writing conferences to show how authors and texts work (see "Create access to complex texts," p. 135).

The most critical piece for teaching reading well is the "right" text. Select books for guided reading, literature discussion, and reading aloud carefully. Do not overrely on preset levels, core reading programs, or textbooks which may have been exclusively written for a school audience rather than a real-world audience. We need to examine the texts ourselves and with our colleagues to determine their readability, suitability for engagement, authenticity, connection to students' lives and cultures, and potential to lead to deep and meaningful discussions. Among other factors, consider length, format and layout (for example, picture book, nonfiction text with charts and graphs, genre) complexity, relevance, and interest level. I like to have at least two selections available so if one turns out not to work with a particular student or group of students, I have an alternative ready to go. With emerging readers, English-language learners, or students who struggle, we may need to write some of these texts with our students in order to fully engage them.

The most critical piece for teaching writing well is the "right" text. Almost every well-known author credits being an avid reader as being the most significant factor in becoming a writer. Yet noticing what authors do and teaching students how to "read like a writer" is frequently a missing piece in our writing curriculum, which we often artificially separate from reading. Use outstanding fiction and nonfiction texts to immerse students in quality texts in various genres—such as poetry, memoir, essay, editorials, commentaries—and demonstrate, point out, explain, and highlight what skillful authors do to hook readers, hold their attention, and convey information in a lively, comprehensible manner. Then, with our guidance, we need to support students as they try out crafting leads, choosing language carefully, writing detailed and clear explanations, adding needed transitions, using punctuation, and much more in a chosen genre or form.

Make no assumptions

I have often taken for granted that students have enough background knowledge and experience to understand the basic vocabulary to understand a read-aloud book, guided reading book, or self-selected book. Then a student will raise his hand and ask, "What does (that word) mean?" and often it is a fundamental word, such as *disappointment* or *energy*. Time and time again, we assume that students—and teachers, too—have general knowledge and experiences about the world or instruction when they do not. For example, almost every time I begin a residency in a new school, the principal and teachers will say something like, "We've had lots of professional development, and we're very 'far along.'" In the past, I assumed the staff was knowledgeable, but I have learned that much professional development is fragmented and superficial, and that we cannot assume anything about what educators do and do not know.

Take action

- **Make it smart to ask questions**. Say something like, "If you don't understand something, a word or idea, raise your hand and ask. Curious people ask questions. That's how we learn." Then, give students—and teachers, too—specific feedback when they follow through. Say something like, "Patrick, I'm glad you said, 'I don't know what revision is' and didn't sit there pretending to understand." Or, "Gloria, a lot of teachers are confused about shared writing. I'm glad you asked about that." Or, "Let's add that question to our list of things we want to find out more about."

- **Find opportunities to demonstrate and apply how to use keywords, concepts, and strategies** until their use is familiar and understood. For example, show, explain, and practice together the "how," "what," and "why" of revision and shared writing. Insert into our daily speaking important words we expect learners to know and apply.

- **Check to be sure basic vocabulary and ideas are understood**. We often assume, often wrongly, that because learners are well behaved and looking right at us that they comprehend what we are teaching. Orally assess before, during, and after instruction. For example, ask and chart, "What do we know about...?" Use that assessment to guide our instruction. Then, as new words, concepts, content, and strategies are learned, add them to the chart. Date each set of entries, using a different color marker each day, to show growing knowledge as well as clarification of confusions and questions. This is a good assessment for teachers as well as students (see "Nurture vocabulary development," p. 107).

♦ **Include discussion of important current events related to issues in the community and in the world**, regardless of the age of our students. We cannot assume, for example, that students know who the president of our country is, the basics of how our government works, or why free elections matter.

Support English-language learners

For all learners, but especially for second-language learners and learners who struggle, we must connect instruction with meaning. Jason was a second-language learner who was struggling mightily in all aspects of literacy. As was the policy for his school and district, he was pulled out of the classroom for ELL support each day. As a result, there was a disconnect between his classroom instruction and the pull-out support he received, and there was scant time for in-depth communication or collaboration with the classroom teacher. Gradually, with daily professional conversations and ongoing, high-quality professional development in her school, Jason's ELL teacher shifted her beliefs and practices from part-to-whole teaching to whole-part-whole teaching (see p. 101). As she witnessed firsthand the greater academic growth that accompanied meaningful instruction, she successfully lobbied her principal to shift to a push-in model for all ELL students. That push-in model built on the same excellent classroom instruction and content all students were receiving. The new model was so successful and joyful that it was replicated throughout the district. Not only that, but many non-ELL students who were also lacking in language skills benefited. We are all learning language all the time and what applies to ELLs also applies universally. We learn language and concepts best through genuine "need to know," meaningful use, supported practice, and relevant interaction (see "Promote oral language development," p. 140).

Take action

- **Build upon students' knowledge, experiences, culture, and interests** to bridge the divide between home and school and to build background knowledge for reading, writing, thinking, and talking in all literacy and content areas.

- **Teach whole to part**, which is a real shift in thinking and beliefs for many ELL teachers. Breaking learning into small pieces makes it harder for ELLs to understand. The parts make most sense in the context of a meaningful whole text or global concept. Of course, we must explicitly teach skills and strategies and ways of thinking, and we temporarily separate these out, and then put them back into context. For example, we explicitly teach vocabulary words, but the words are in service to understanding a text, concept, or idea and are not part of an isolated list.

- **State clearly the language goals and purpose for the instruction**. State all objectives and directions succinctly and unambiguously; check to make sure students understand the learning goals for the content and language. Say something like, "At the end of the lesson, we're going to check and find evidence of what we've learned."

- **Ask significant questions** (see p. 12). Although ELLs may not yet be able to read and write at the highest levels, they can think at high levels if we expect it, scaffold our teaching so that the language and content are comprehensible, and ask important questions (see "Promote significant conversations," p. 129).

- **Involve as many senses as possible**. The more comprehensible we make the input, the easier it is to learn. ELLs need to hear it, see it, experience it, feel it, talk about it, and have physical involvement, wherever possible. For example, a class of kindergarten students wrote and performed their own raps for learning phonics rimes, such as i-n-g: "See me jumping- i-n-g. When am I doing it? Right now!" Raps were performed and celebrated schoolwide! In the past, the ELL teacher in this story would have told her students, "We're working on present tense verbs." Now, she said, "We're going to write a rap in order to learn about action words, also called *verbs*, which we do 'right now.'"

- **Advocate for best practices**. Current research shows that second-language learners benefit most from dual language programs and intentional, real-world instruction. As well, work towards push-in models and minimize pull-out models (see p. 140).

Create a need to know

Acclaimed director James Cameron begins his movie *Titanic* with video footage on the ship's sinking. In 2012, he revisits the facts that informed his 1995 conclusions and asks: "What could have happened?" "What actually happened?" "Why did it happen?" Cameron still had so many unanswered questions on a topic he was passionate about that, with a team of experts, he investigated, once again, the possible causes and explanations for the quick sinking and extensive damage to the ship. The "need to know" drove him to explore and scrutinize further, reanalyze all the facts, and reach new conclusions. That intense curiosity is exactly what we want to foster in our students—and ourselves.

When I ask a group of students, "What do we mean by revision?" there is no response and not much interest in knowing. The teacher has been assigning most writing in the classroom and directed any changes to be made, so, not surprisingly, most students don't value writing or see a connection between in-school writing and real-world writing. Without a need to know, in this case, knowing what revision is and why it matters, students will not improve much as writers and thinkers. Telling teaching, where we give the explanations and solutions to students, has been shown to be far less effective than responsive teaching, where through our thoughtful questioning, probing, and interaction with students, we create a need for inquiry. Although we may be restrained by required curriculum and standards, we must present content in a way that entices a hunger to know more, which, in turn creates the motivation, engagement, and persistence that lead to new and lasting learning.

Take action

- **Find out what students are passionate about and "need to know."** Encourage investigation of a topic of interest. Provide excellent resources.

- **Demonstrate the research process** and how one comes to an informed opinion. Follow the Optimal Learning Model (see p. 15).

- **Value uncertainty**. By the types of questions we pose (see "Ask more vital questions," p. 12) we challenge students' thinking. Not relying on one perfect answer promotes curiosity and a continuous desire to learn. Begin, as James Cameron did, with these essential questions: "What do we know now?" Then, after some investigation, "What have we learned?" Next, "What else do we want to find out?" and "How can we find that information?" Finally, "What are our conclusions, based on all the evidence and analysis?"

- ◆ **Challenge students' thinking**. Rather than giving students "the answer," ask, "What do you think?" or "How could we find that out?" Explicitly demonstrate and show how curious people find information to their questions so that, with our guidance, students can search, browse, read, research, and collaborate to find answers to their questions.

- ◆ **Pose our own "need to know" questions**. For example, investigate and problem solve such possible issues as to why so many students are being labeled for special education, why the writing at two adjacent grade levels looks about the same, why so few students reach proficiency level in reading, or what are our specific burning question(s) for ourselves or our school for maximizing achievement, engagement, and more.

Enjoy teaching

Teachers say we don't have time for joy. In too many schools, the pressure to raise achievement is relentless. The required high-stakes testing, teacher evaluation, program mandates, implementation of the latest standards, and curriculum demands sap our energy and pleasure. Yet without joy in our daily teaching we cannot be highly effective. Plain and simple, it's difficult to be great at something we don't like doing. Sadly, I have never been invited to do a reading or writing residency in a school because the kids hate and fear writing or dislike reading, although that is often the case. In almost every instance where I have been invited to a school, it is to "to raise the test scores." Our national obsession with testing is like a disease gone viral. It is out of control, damaging, and hard to cure.

It is the joy of teaching and learning, highly visible to school members by the end of a teaching residency—the sheer pleasure and energy burst that come from teaching authentically and purposefully—that drives us to do better and to enjoy teaching more. One teacher commented, "When you talked about the joy factor at the beginning of the residency, many of us rolled our eyes. We were thinking, 'We don't have time for that joy thing.' We had curriculum to cover, lessons to plan, and district mandates to worry about. But, by the end of the week, we saw that that joy thing was everything."

Take action

+ **Reevaluate how we spend planning and instructional time**, for example:

  - Do we really need to have long writing projects, which place high demands on us for conferring, revising, and editing, or can we teach what students need to know with shorter assignments?

  - Are the projects and management we are creating for students worth the time and effort they take? Can we simplify those and still maintain high quality? Is students' constant dependence on us sapping our energy and joy?

  - Do we really need to have guided reading groups with all students every day, or might we be more effective and enjoy teaching more if we allowed more time for closely monitored independent reading and daily conferring?

- **Take more time to celebrate small victories** and notice and comment on what students and staff are doing well. Seeing a student's or teacher's face light up with an "I can do it" spirit inspires us and our students to work harder and set challenging goals.

- **Leave school at a reasonable hour**, and try not to take much work home, so we have time for those activities that bring us pleasure and peace of mind.

- **Plan occasions for the staff to socialize**. Potluck lunches, snacking on special treats before a PD meeting, and specially planned events outside of school can all contribute to the staff getting to know each other better, which makes work time more enjoyable.

- **Recognize that change takes time**. Try not to be too hard on ourselves when lessons fail, we err in judgment, or misstep. Becoming a more effective teacher, leader, and learner is a lifelong process. Take credit and pleasure in recognizing and analyzing our errors and then finding ways to do better.

Write more short pieces

Encouraging short writing assignments makes writing easier for students and us. We can teach students everything they need to know about writing, such as leads, organization, word choice, elaboration and detail, closure, revision, and editing with a short writing piece. A nonfiction report does not need to be many pages long, which can drain students' energy as well as our own. Even for older students, think about demonstrating, practicing, and assigning shorter pieces and assigning only one or two big writing projects a year. Shorter writing pieces, for authentic audiences and purposes, can move writing from being burdensome to being everyone's favorite subject.

Take action

- **Demonstrate only the amount of writing that most students are capable of doing at this time**. Write and think aloud in front of our students, use shared writing, or show student writing exemplars. Be conscious of not taking valuable time—as well as students' energy and sustained time needed for actual writing—by demonstrating too much, for example, when we model two pages of writing when most students are typically writing one page.

- **Bring a piece of writing to a final, published copy at least once a month, starting in grade 2 and above**. Students need lots of practice in revising and editing if they are to become proficient writers, and short assignments make that possible.

- **Consider some of the following short writing forms and genres**:
  - Letters (thank you, gratitude, persuasive, request, editorial)
  - Reviews (book, restaurant, magazine, video, play, movie, game, app)
  - Notes (birthday, congratulations, holiday greeting)
  - All about the author (student profile to be attached to published writing)
  - Capturing a moment (honing in on one small part of an incident to bring it to life) in a piece of writing
  - Poetry writing, free verse
  - Developing a character (as a prelude to fiction writing)
  - Picture books for younger readers

See *Writing Essentials* (Routman, 2005) for many more ideas and examples.

Use technology judiciously

Iconfess: I've been slow to apply new technologies to my teaching. Unlike my granddaughters who are growing up with these new literacies like a second language in which they are fluent, I bumble along and need hand-holding every step of the way. Still, I am a convert. I know that the right technology tools can help do our jobs better and make our teaching more interactive, motivating, and self-directing for us and our students. I recently took a leap of faith and began doing presentations to large and small groups using my iPad, connected wirelessly. My goal was not to use the latest technology but to communicate more effectively with my audience, and an iPad makes that possible. With fewer barriers between the audience and me, I feel I can be more personal and conversational, which is my desired presentation style.

For our students, too, meaningful purpose must accompany technology use. Access to videos such as YouTube for Schools, wise use of social media, smartboards and document cameras, interactive Internet formats, film, e-textbooks that can be continually updated, podcasts, webcasts, various art forms, blogs, wikis, student-made videos, school and district websites, live chats with people across the globe, and more offer us possibilities for making teaching and learning more dynamic, engaging, and efficient. Our students and we have unlimited options for accessing information, uniquely expressing ourselves, and communicating. Still, there is a caution. Computers, tablets, videos, computerized programs, e-readers, and other devices do not guarantee better learning. The goal is not more technology use but more effective, engaged, and accelerated teaching and learning. Technology, when it is used wisely, has the potential to fulfill that goal.

Take action

◆ **Use technology to communicate more effectively:**

- Create classroom, school, and district websites. Publish book reviews and newsletters to parents, which include subject matter work and commentaries by students. Create a welcome packet for new students and their families (see "Infuse the arts into teaching and learning," p. 154).

- Have students, with our guidance and presentation software, make a class-authored PowerPoint presentation for the school server to teach other students, parents, or community members a concept or content.

- Establish online blogs and other formats that provide information and perspectives on science experiments and observations, community studies, and key political and social issues, and more.
- Access outstanding websites, such as www.edutopia.org and www.ReadWriteThink.org for inspiration, innovation, information, and excellent resources to support our curriculum and instruction.
- Post student and class-made videos that explain content learning and thinking across the curriculum.
- Create a tutorial in language that is clear and concise to help parents understand the latest standards, report cards, homework guidelines, school rules, and so on.
- Do our demonstration writing using a document camera. The document camera also works extremely well for public conferences (see p. 78)— after the student has read the writing at least once and we focus on content and for public editing conferences, as well.
- Send persuasive letters and editorials to local and national newspapers, school boards, and national organizations.

- **Embed technology that increases student engagement and motivation**. Consider novel uses for Twitter and other social media, for example, having students compose book reviews or summaries limited to 140 characters. Explore the possible use of e-publishing, digital books, and websites such as Edutopia, which can provide interactive diagrams, audio and video tools, and technological flourishes that illuminate and enhance content and concepts.
- **Ensure that the technology we use is worth our time**. It's easy to turn responsibility over to a computerized program or electronic device and assume, perhaps falsely, that students are progressing and learning more. Be sure we can reliably assess everything we ask students to do.

Do more frontloading

There is nothing more frustrating and time consuming than having to re-teach a lesson because we haven't given students enough useful demonstrations and experiences to guarantee their success. It happens to the best of us. In almost every case, where many students have experienced difficulties, they are directly related to how much frontloading I've done. Frontloading means the assessing-before-teaching, modeling, explanations, shared experiences, providing of background knowledge, preteaching vocabulary when needed, scaffolded conversations (see p. 104 for explanation), partner and small-group work, and everything we do to make it likely that *all* learners succeed when they attempt to apply what we have been teaching them. Frontloading is as important for us teachers and leaders as it is for our students. Too often we are expected to apply new programs, standards, curriculum, and more without sufficient frontloading.

Take action

- **Provide sufficient demonstrations**. Regardless of the behavior, skill, action, task, strategy we want students to be able to do well, we have to demonstrate exactly what we expect. We not only need to show students how to do the task or activity; we need to make our in-the-head thinking and problem solving visible to them (see "Do more demonstrations," p. 19).

- **Check to be sure students understood and learned from our demonstrations** before we move on. Depending on students' responses, we may need to repeat the demonstration before they are ready to try out the task or activity. Have students explain the task they are about to undertake through turn and talk with a partner or discussion in a small group. Then call on anyone in the group to explain the task.

- **Use shared experiences** such as creating charts and rubrics together ("What did you notice me do in the demonstration?"), conducting public scaffolded conversations with students, and providing time for small-group work before releasing students to work on their own.

◆ **Provide additional frontloading** as needed. Even when we have done our best, it's typical to have a small group of students who need more frontloading, for example, our students who struggle, our English-language learners, and those low in confidence. Pull them aside while the rest of the class gets to work. Then, when conferring-on-the-run, check in with these students first to ensure they're off to a good start, which can save reteaching, boost students' confidence, and give them energy to continue working.

Acknowledge an unexpected hero

In life and in work, there are times when someone steps up to the plate for us when we least expect it. It might be someone who stands up for us in a difficult situation or who magnanimously offers to do something that's needed. Our schools and classrooms are positively affected by the good deeds of unexpected heroes, and we need to recognize and appreciate even the smallest of kind gestures. In fact, a thriving school culture depends on each of us making a concerted effort for others, which includes "being there" when the going gets rough. My Uncle Harry was that person for me. When my father had a debilitating stroke at the age of 85, cousin Harry, known to all of us in the family as Uncle Harry, showed up at the hospital wearing his beloved New York Yankees cap. Among his first words to me were, "If anything happens to your dad, I'll take care of the funeral service. Don't pay anyone to do it." I was taken aback because Uncle Harry was 93.

My dad's gradual rehabilitation was slow and wrenching, and after several years, Dad's old and dear friends disappeared but Uncle Harry stayed the course, just about the only one to do so. Every two weeks for more than seven years, he wrote a heartfelt, newsy letter—which was also meant for me—as I had to read it aloud to my dad. Uncle Harry's letters included the news of the day; participation in events with family, friends, and his girlfriend; his driving adventures; reminiscences on long-ago outings with my mom and dad; and, always an off-color joke at the end that made us laugh. Those precious letters became a lifeline of hope for Dad and me. One of his later letters included big news and newspaper clippings with photos: Somehow, Uncle Harry's beloved New York Yankees found out that his upcoming 99th birthday coincided with the opening day of their new stadium and that Uncle Harry, at age 13, had been present on the original stadium's opening day. On his birthday, courtesy of the Yankees organization, he was picked up in a white stretch limousine, taken to the new stadium, and seated in a place of honor. At intermission, he was interviewed on the big screen for all to see, and tens of thousands sang Happy Birthday to him. Uncle Harry couldn't have been prouder.

My proud moment came a year later when, at the age of 100, he conducted a beautiful and intimate service at my dad's funeral. It was a blustery, March day in New York, and Uncle Harry was the only one without a coat. Still firm of step and quick of mind, he spoke eloquently of my dad and their long and close friendship. Uncle Harry taught me the importance of staying in touch and showing up for people you care about, even when it's hard to do so. At this writing, he is 102, still active and independent and telling jokes. Through phone calls and letters, I continue to let him know how much his caring example meant to my dad and me.

Take action

- **Show appreciation to our unsung heroes**. When someone "steps up" to make a worthy difference for us, whether it's a grounder or a home run, let that person know. Have students write letters or communications of gratitude to a family member, former teacher, friend, or significant person in their lives describing a special moment, act, or action that has affected them. Model first with our own letter, perhaps, to a colleague who has done something very supportive and unexpected. Next, write one together, and construct a simple rubric with students (see p. 99) before sending them off to write their letters.

- **Celebrate daily acts of kindness by school community members**—crossing guards, bus drivers, volunteers, secretaries, curriculum directors, families, students, teachers, administrators, parents, and more. Through oral and written communications and heartfelt "thank yous," acknowledge the thoughtful acts.

Teach with a sense of urgency

Teaching with a sense of urgency means focusing relentlessly on what's most important every single day throughout the day, moving at an efficient and effective steady pace, seizing problems and failure as opportunities for growth, and changing course as needed to maximize learning. It does not mean speeding up lessons to teach faster; in fact, it may mean slowing down to teach more deeply so students are more successful when they attempt a task—which saves time in the long run.

Take action

- **Keep the flow of teaching going** through purposeful, engaging, and relevant lessons that connect to students' interests and needs as well as to required curriculum and standards.

- **Stop while energy is still high** and the students and we can come back to the lesson with energy and excitement.

- **Try not to stop teaching for off-task behaviors**; when possible, move a student right up next to us with a statement like, "Chris, come right up to the front. I need someone to help me with..."

- **Do away with unnecessary routines, rules, and procedures** that take lots of time but don't move learning forward, for example, creating and posting classroom charts in academic language that students cannot understand and access.

- **Eliminate distractions** (see p. 94).

- **Do more frontloading** (see p. 73).

- **Be efficient** in our directions and the language we use. Be concise, clear, and explicit.

Embrace public writing conferences

Conferring with students is the single best way I know to move them forward as writers. From kindergarten through high school, students greatly benefit from seeing and hearing the language of conferring. In a public conference, one student has a conference with the teacher in full view of the whole class or group while the other students are looking on, listening, and thinking about how to apply to their own writing what they are learning. Begin with content conferences. Editing doesn't matter much if the writing is not worth reading. Also important to keep in mind, students cannot effectively confer with peers until we have demonstrated and they have tried out, with our guidance, the helpful language and actions of conferring.

Take action

- **Be explicit in how and why the public conference can benefit all students.** Say something like, "We are having this public conference for two reasons. First, we're going to celebrate what the writer has done well. It's your job to listen closely to be sure you have done those same kinds of things in your own writing. Second, we may give the writer some suggestions. Again, you want to pay close attention, as I will expect you to reread your paper and make some revisions based on what applies to your own writing."

- **Have the first public conference with a strong writer**, so we have a good role model for other students, the work to be done is manageable, and we feel successful.

- **Have the student read the piece aloud first**, if he is willing. On the first reading, try not to look at the writing (which can lead us to focus on grammar, legibility, or poor spelling) and listen for the whole message of what the writer is trying to say. If the piece is long, have the writer orally say what the piece is about; then have him choose one part where he wants feedback.

- **Read the paper aloud a second time**—and third time, if needed—to think on our feet and go by line by line to specifically name the exact language, craft, structure, organization, and so on that the writer has used to affect the reader and convey his message.

- **Go line by line and celebrate everything the writer has done well**. Choose our language carefully, and focus on the actual words the student has used and what those words convey. It is not helpful to the writer or to other students listening in to say, "I like your beginning" or "You used good detail" because we don't know what that means and can't emulate it. It is helpful to say, "Listen to Sarah's first lines (and read the exact language aloud) and notice the way her words and rhythm entice the reader into the story. Make sure you have done something similar with your own writing."

- **Decide on what's most important to say and do at this time to move the writer forward**, and make one or two teaching points, for example, cutting and pasting for organization, writing a better lead, or both. Remember that sometimes, the writing is "good enough" as it is. Especially for writers who struggle, we want the writer to leave the conference with the energy, confidence, and will to do any necessary revision and editing work.

- **Make conferring manageable**. Do one or two in-depth public conferences. Do not worry if such a conference takes 15 or 20 minutes. Remember that "less is more" when we want students to think and apply techniques at a deep and meaningful level.

- **Ensure the language we use can be understood**. Not only are we seeking to have students apply what we are celebrating and suggesting, but also we are also modeling the language of response for worthwhile peer conferences.

Provide feedback that supports the learner

I will never forget walking into a primary-grade teacher's classroom and her enthusiastically saying, "What do you think of my word wall?" It filled the entire length of her classroom and had more than 200 words on it. "What do you want to know?" I asked her. She went on to talk about how carefully she had designed the wall and how proud of it she was. It was clear from her comments and demeanor that what she wanted was praise and validation for her hard work. So I honestly told her, "It's very colorful and beautiful. I can tell you've put a lot of effort into it. It's the first thing I noticed when I entered your room." She beamed.

A year later, when I was back in her classroom, she asked me again, "What do you think of my word wall?" and, again, I responded, "What do you want to know?" This time she said, "I think I may have way too many words up for the kids, and some of the words are placed so high I'm wondering if students can access them." Now she was ready to improve the quality of the word wall and see it as a useful literacy tool. So I told her, "Your word wall is beautiful, but it does seem like you have too many words up. I worry about kids who will be overwhelmed by how many words are there. Also, I wonder if you've thought about just having one word to represent a common rime, such as *-ake*, for example, and just having the word *make* up there and color coding *-ake* to let students know that if they know *make* they can figure out *take* and *wake*. Also, for those keywords that everyone can read and spell, you might consider taking those down." I did feel she needed to lower the word wall to be at eye level for most of the students, but I focused my feedback on what seemed easily doable and, most important, at this time, to help her improve the word wall without overwhelming her. At a later date, I could add the other suggestion.

Feedback, to be useful, must use carefully crafted language that helps the learner improve the quality of the work. The learner must also be ready to receive the constructive suggestion(s). That is why celebration, which we have already discussed, is a necessary precursor to feedback. Feedback, thoughtfully delivered, gives the learner agency and energy to move forward. Finally, feedback needs to be immediate, to be most helpful to the learner.

Word wall feedback story is adapted from *Teaching Essentials* (Routman, 2008a, p. 44).

Take action

- **Focus first on the learner and, second, on the learning that is needed**. Be thinking: "What is the most important thing I can say to this learner that will empower him to move forward and give him the energy to do the work?"

- **Give positive feedback on what the learner has done well before making suggestions**. Learners first need to hear at least several positive statements focused on specific behaviors and actions.

- **Limit comments to the task at hand**. Be thinking: "What is the learner ready and willing to hear now to improve the work?" See specific language to the teacher in the word wall aforementioned story for one example.

- **Give feedback in specific language the learner can understand**. Be thinking: "How can I say this in a way that is positive, comprehensible, and useful?"

- **Use language that will encourage the learner to take action**. For example, we might say something like, "Carlos, let's review what we both agree you can do on your own. When you go back to your seat, carefully reread, refer to the brief comments we put on the sticky notes to remind you of actions to take and words to use. I'll be by after a while to check on how you're doing."

- **Check to be sure the learner has understood the feedback**. Have the learner say back what he or she has just heard.

Read and write more texts

Quantity matters. If we are able to assess all the pages students read and write, they're not reading and writing enough. Students need to be reading and writing authentic and continuous texts for uninterrupted and sustained periods of time every day. Research has unequivocally shown that students in high-challenge schools can become unexpectedly high achieving when their teachers and they are reading and writing numerous relevant and engaging texts, each day, applying authentic and engaging literacy practices, and doing a minimal amount of activities *about* reading and writing. (Allington, 2002; Taylor, Pearson, Peterson, & Rodriguez, 2002).

Take action

- **Count the number of texts we read to and with students each day**. For younger students aim for at least 6–10 texts a day. A text is defined as a read-aloud, a shared reading, a rereading of a class-authored text, reading of student-authored text, reading of a chart, and so on.

- **Make sustained reading and writing time a priority**. It's in this "practice" stage that students attempt to apply what we are teaching them, experiment with language, figure out new vocabulary, notice what authors do, reread for clarity, gain fluency, build stamina, self-monitor, and much more.

- **Emphasize reading and writing authentic texts**, and minimize isolated passages and excerpts without sufficient context for understanding.

- **Publish more class-authored and student-authored work**. Publish these into individual books and collections that students can reread throughout the day and school year. For all learners, but especially for our English-language learners and students who struggle, stories and texts about their lives, interests, and culture—in their own words—are always the easiest for them to read and understand.

- **Save a variety of exemplary, student-authored texts**. Have students keep their "first edition" and make "second editions" with students' permission. Put these in the classroom library for before-school reading and independent reading time. Also, as we begin a new school year, we have lots of student- and class-authored texts in the classroom library—for high interest reading texts and as writing models.

- **Lessen summer reading loss**. Send home booklets for each student with most or all of the class-authored texts and shared reading pieces and poems bound together. Include directions for families that encourage rereading of texts for fluency and enjoyment. Seek out ways to ensure students participate in some type of summer reading program, for example, open the school library several times throughout the summer for book checkout.

Focus on the essential ingredients

I recently finished a delightful book of fiction, *The School of Essential Ingredients* by Erica Bauermeister (2009). The main character runs a cooking school, and on the first night of class, she tells her students, "I might as well tell you, there isn't a list and I've never had one. Nor do I hand out recipes. All I can say is you will learn what you need to..." (pp. 43–44). It's not much different for becoming a highly effective literacy teacher.

When I first started going into schools to do demonstration teaching and coaching of reading and writing practices in classrooms, teachers would typically ask, "Can you give me a list of all the skills I need to teach, preferably, in the order I should teach them?" At the end of the weeklong residency, we would make a list of all the skills we'd taught, and teachers were amazed at how many more skills we had "covered" when we focused first on meaningful teaching (see "Apply whole-part-whole teaching," p. 101) and embedded the skills that were needed into the instructional context. Literally, our skills list was pages long!

Of course, there is no one "right" list, and there is no research to support a "correct" hierarchy for teaching reading and writing skills. Some publishers would have us believe that if we follow a core program and teach a set of skills and strategies in a prescribed order, students will become literate. Not likely. Programs don't teach. We teachers do. At best, a core program provides an important beginning framework that can help us build a necessary foundation, but a program is insufficient for ongoing, highly effective teaching.

Some of the essential ingredients for becoming an expert literacy teacher include, but are not limited to:

- Focusing first on our students as unique individuals and second on what we need to teach them
- Being an active participator in a collaborative, professional learning community
- Becoming professionally knowledgeable about literacy and learning
- Knowing how to engage all our students
- Seeking out mentoring and coaching experiences
- Being open to change
- Finding joy in teaching and learning

None of this is easy. It's a lifelong journey, which is why I call myself a learner–teacher, and not the other way around.

Teach less, learn more

Those four words are the mantra and logo for Singapore Schools, one of the best in the world according to international comparisons. The Ministry of Education notes, "Teach Less, Learn More is about teaching better, to engage our learners and prepare them for life, rather than teaching more, for tests and examinations." Teachers and students aim to adopt of mind-set of quality interaction in and beyond the classroom. If we were to customize our educational practices to truly meet the diverse needs of our students, our schools would look very different from what they do today. We would know our students and their families better, we would teach life skills as well as literacy skills, instill self-evaluation abilities, support students in project-based learning, have more embedded time for increasing professional knowledge—on our own and with our colleagues, and we and our school leaders would have more authority and courage to initiate changes to serve our students better.

Here's what we can do. We can become terrifically knowledgeable so when the next set of standards, mandates, and curriculum come along, as they always do, we can use those new guidelines and resources as an informational framework, not as a recipe, dictate, or manual to be rigidly followed. We can take responsibility for promoting professional conversations throughout the school and district—in both horizontal and vertical structures. We can make teaching and learning decisions that are best for our students—based on reliable research, our own teaching experiences and growing knowledge, and students' needs, backgrounds, and interests. We can and must speak up, advocate for, and instill saner practices and wiser use of existing resources—even if we have to close our doors to apply sensible practices and use resources more effectively and intelligently.

Expect correct spelling and conventions

A group of proud students gave me a copy of their monthly class newsletter for parents. The content was excellent, full of interesting and well-written information about the goings-on of the class—what they had been learning, doing, and thinking about. Here's what I told them after I carefully read the newsletter: "Your newsletter is excellent. You have engaging leads, great descriptions, and you communicate information clearly. I can tell you are serious writers. However, I was distracted by the spelling and punctuation errors. As a reader, I count on correctness so I can focus on the message." They "got it." From that point on, many students took responsibility for rereading the newsletter. They challenged me to find errors, and I never did. Correct spelling, conventions, and grammar are about respect for the reader. Readers expect and deserve a seamless read to focus on meaning.

Take action

- **Emphasize that writers write for readers**. Just like the students in the aforementioned story, once students internalize that we write for a purpose and a valued audience—beyond the bulletin board or teacher—they take spelling and correct conventions seriously.

- **Raise expectations**. Ensure that whatever goes public is as perfect as possible. That's how it is in the world, and that's how it needs to be in school. Poor spelling and conventions reflect poorly on us as teachers and send a message to the public that spelling doesn't matter much. From early on in grade 2, almost all students are capable of "fixing up" basic spelling and conventions if we expect them to do it, teach explicitly, and give lots of guided practice through writing and publishing for authentic purposes and audiences.

- **Expect high-frequency words to be spelled correctly**. Even in a draft, expect word-wall words and agreed-upon high-frequency words to be spelled correctly. When they are not, put a penciled mark or symbol above the word to indicate the student is expected to fix-up that word.

- **Place responsibility for editing on the students**. Only confer with students about editing once they have done, on their own or with peer assistance, everything they know how to do regarding correct spelling and conventions.

Hold firm! We disable students, in the long run, when we do for them what they can do on their own or with peer assistance.

- **Explain invented spelling**. For younger students, in kindergarten and grade 1, if we post work with invented spellings—especially in school hallways—be sure to accompany that work with a notice that says something like, "Our best independent spelling" or something to that effect, so readers and the public know we are doing our job. Invented spellings are appropriate for those words we do not yet expect students to be able to spell and for encouraging the use of unique vocabulary so that students do not feel limited to basic, easy-to-spell words.

- **Provide student-friendly resources**, such as word walls, personal "word walls" in students' writing folders or notebooks, small dictionaries with high-frequency words, and so on.

Resist teaching to the test

With extreme pressure on teachers, principals, and schools to raise test scores, it's understandable that we would feel a need to teach to the test. We want to do what's best and we don't want to let anyone down, not the school, the students, and not ourselves. Here's one sobering truth: The side effects of excessive test prep can be extremely harmful. Scores might go up, but students do not necessarily learn more. In fact, what they and their teachers do learn may actually set them back. What follows is a cautionary tale.

Panic was evident on the faces of the conscientious, fourth-grade teachers—the high-stakes testing grade—on the very first day of a writing residency. My best efforts to calm teachers down had little impact. I told them something like, "The interim writing assessments we just did indicate that fourth graders are, typically, more than two years below grade level. We can't make that up in one year. So focus on excellent teaching of writing, not test prep. Remember that having fourth graders do well on the test is the responsibility of the whole school, not just the fourth grade team." The fourth-grade teachers tried to take my advice, but they didn't yet believe that spending most of their time on highly effective teaching was the surest route to raising achievement. Their beliefs about teaching writing were still evolving, and, for now, they believed that intensive test prep meant the best chance for improved writing scores. It would take more than a year for teachers to come to believe and to put into practice: If we focus on the process, the product will improve.

At the end of the school year, most fourth graders had made minimal test gains, and their attitudes about writing had become negative. In an interview with the teachers and the students, almost every student indicated that because of constant attention to the test prep writing and ongoing focus on directed writing prompts, they and the teacher had lost enthusiasm for writing. The joy of writing, which we had experienced when we all worked together in the fall, was gone. Not only that, but students' everyday writing overall showed no improvement from fall to spring. It would take months of soul searching by the teachers for that joy to return, along with improved quality of student writing. The excessive test-prep focus came with a high cost.

Take action

◆ **Keep test prep to a minimum**. A month before the test, familiarize students with the test format, test-taking strategies, and practice test exercises. Show students the rubric, in a student-friendly version, that the state uses to score tests. Have students self-evaluate their practice tests with our guidance and set goals for improvement, if needed.

◆ **Maintain focus on expert teaching**. Make connections to test-taking through our daily language and ongoing writing work. For example, I might say something like, "Today, when we heard Maria read her piece, we noticed how she let the reader know when she was changing topics. She said, 'Here's what we do next.' We call that guidance to the reader a 'transition.' In your own writing, and when you take the state test, be sure to use transitions when needed."

◆ **Inform parents**. Let families know that a standardized test is just one measure of their child's progress. Frequently share day-to-day formative assessments (see p. 145) so families have a complete picture and can put high stakes tests in perspective.

Remain hopeful

For as long as I have been teaching, the educational climate has been challenging, and will, no doubt, remain so. High-stakes testing, standards, curriculum mandates, new programs, and the politics of literacy continue to play a commanding role in making teaching, coaching, and leading very professionally and personally demanding. Yet if we focus our energies on our students, where we can and must make a crucial difference in their literacy lives, we can have a positive impact on them, one student at a time. Although the educational system is broken in too many places, and repairing it through school reform efforts is beyond most of our control, school change is possible in our own classrooms and schools, one student at a time.

We must make an all-out effort to discard the harmful, excuses mentality and mind-set so often prevalent in schools where students come from poverty, are second-language learners, or have some other designated label. For the many hours a day we have our students, we must take full responsibility for educating them to the fullest and giving them all the opportunities that a first class education can provide.

Many of us have stories of students whose lives have been changed by our teaching. Countless times, I have seen a child who saw himself as incapable change before our eyes in a public conference where we celebrated his strengths. Our impact can be lifelong. A former student, who had been a struggling reader, recently phoned out of the blue to say, "Thirty years ago, you taught me how to read and changed my life. I just want to thank you for not giving up on me." We are the lifeline of hope and possibilities for so many of our students. We are the keepers of their dreams.

Design and assign appropriate homework

While the research on homework has been clear and uncontested for at least five decades, because many of us are unfamiliar with it, the debate rages on. Harris Cooper (2006), the country's most esteemed homework researcher, has compiled and analyzed the most comprehensive studies on homework and concludes, "too much homework may diminish its effectiveness or even be counterproductive" (p. 26). He recommends that homework per grade level be assigned only on Monday through Thursday, with 10 minutes a night in grade 1, 20 minutes in grade 2 and so on, gradually increasing to one to two hours a night through the high school years.

Consider homework to be the practice phase, that is, students already know how "to do it" reasonably well. The best homework extends and solidifies the learning, builds good study habits, and helps students feel more competent and confident. Two of my favorite, worthwhile homework assignments for K–6 students are reading a self-selected book or portion of a book, and coming prepared to write—through prethinking and, perhaps, jotting down ideas—about an authentic writing topic that we have already discussed and demonstrated.

Take action

- **Develop a schoolwide, homework policy that is sane, sensible, and equitable**. Assigned work must not depend on parents and family members' assistance for students to be successful. Too many of the families we serve do not have the time, energy, or skills to guide their children. Be sure to clearly communicate the school's homework policy and suggest reasonable ways families can support their children.

- **Make homework manageable** for students and their families, with clear guidelines that are easy enough for students to explain to their parents. For example, at the end of each week, have kindergarten and first-grade students take home a shared writing that they have reread many times in school and, now, can proudly read to their families. On the reverse side of the paper, as an assessment before the paper goes home, we can ask students to write a few high-frequency words that come from the text. Students will have talked about and practiced these words all week including how to self-check and self-correct them. Parents see content that has been taught that week along with embedded word work, and even our youngest students can explain what they are learning. Another example, for older students, is to have them keep a reading response journal, which can be used later to write a book review or summary.

Share inspiring stories

If we want our students excited about reading and writing, we must read, tell, and write interesting stories and texts to engage and inspire them. Nothing holds our students' attention more than a well-told story. It's why the first thing I do when I work in a new classroom is to share stories. Typically, I read a terrific nonfiction or fiction book that connects to our curriculum and students' lives. I also tell stories from my life and enthusiastically pull out all the stops when doing so.

Take action

- **Seek out the very best nonfiction and fiction literature** and bring those texts into the classroom—as read-alouds, inspiration for further reading and writing, part of the classroom library, models for our own demonstration writing, and models for showing and noticing what authors do. A few highly recommended picture books for older and younger readers are Herb Shoveller's *Ryan and Jimmy: And the Well in Africa That Brought Them Together*, Kirby Lawson's and Mary Nethery's *Two Bobbies: A True Story of Hurricane Katrina, Friendship, and Survival*, Jennifer Holland's *Unlikely Friendships: 47 Remarkable Stories From the Animal Kingdom*, and Pam Muñoz Ryan's *When Marian Sang: The True Recital of Marian Anderson*.

- **Choose stories that inspire hope.** Students living in poverty or with hardships need to hear and read true stories of people, like themselves, who overcame overwhelming odds. See the "I Can Do It!" booklist under Text Resources on the *Teaching Essentials* website for many excellent nonfiction picture books that serve as role models of people who struggled mightily but went on to make significant contributions.

- **Include the elaboration and details from our oral story telling** when we are demonstration writing; do not just write a bare bones story. Put meat on the bones! To accomplish that, we may need to choose to focus on just one moment or part of the story when we write.

- **Read book reviews and book-related websites, frequent bookstores, get to know librarians** and seek out their recommendations, find out what genres students prefer, and share the latest and "best" books and texts.

Eliminate distractions

If we are to teach with a sense of urgency, we must do all we can to minimize whole-school and classroom disruptions that impede instruction and learning. There is nothing so frustrating as to be in the flow of an effective lesson only to have bells or buzzers go off or have an inconsequential announcement come over the public address system. We lose not only our pace, thoughts, and momentum, but also we lose precious time. Just 10 minutes a day of unproductive time adds up to about 3.5 hours a month!

Take action

- **Advocate for reducing teaching interruptions**:

  - Take time at a staff meeting to have a dialogue on how to lessen non-essential, schoolwide, daily interruptions.

  - Eliminate or greatly shorten announcements over the public address system as much as possible. For example, instead of a P.A. announcement stating a student needs to come to the office, try to work out a system where a messenger delivers the request, orally or in writing, at least some of the time.

- **Have students take more responsibility for solving classroom-based issues**. Use shared writing to brainstorm solutions for typical social and learning problems in the classroom. The shift to student-in-charge from teacher-in-charge of problem solving requires guided discussion. Originally, most students in a grade 2–3 classroom placed "Tell the teacher" at the top of their list as the first and only solution for an ongoing problem, "Students annoying you when you are trying to do your work." Their "Solutions" on the first draft of the class-authored shared writing quickly expanded with "Tell the teacher" moving to the last resort:

  - Ignore them (do not talk back).
  - Tell them to stop.
  - Work it out with the person who is bothering you. Say, "Can you please stop bothering me?"
  - Walk away.

- Move your sheet away. ("Sheet" refers to the stand-up folder some students use on their desks to have more privacy as they work.)
- Tell the teacher.

◆ **Make expectations clear and prominent**. The aforementioned student solutions—along with solutions to other pressing problems—remained posted for the school year. Because students identified workable solutions, compliance was high. In those few instances where there was a lapse, the teacher only needed to briefly refer to the chart to keep students' undivided attention on their work, which meant she could instruct small groups or work one-on-one with students, uninterrupted. In another classroom where the teacher and students discussed appropriate behaviors towards each other, students worked together to create character education posters.

Teach handwriting

Handwriting still matters—a lot. There. I've said it. In school after school and classroom after classroom, the writing of far too many students is undecipherable, sloppy, and done without pride. Poor handwriting is an epidemic that is adversely affecting students' writing fluency, stamina, competence, and writing confidence. We disadvantage students when they cannot and do not form letters properly, hold the pencil or pen awkwardly, or both. Many students are now writing slower and composing shorter, hard to read, pieces—primarily because they have not been taught handwriting. Sadly, once students have established incorrect habits for letter formation, it can be very difficult to reteach them, even in grade 1!

The solution is an easy one. We need to teach handwriting, formally and informally, beginning early in kindergarten. Somewhere along the way, many of us got the message that we should leave students alone to form letters and hold the pencil as best they could and not interfere. We are now seeing the results of those misguided beliefs.

Take action

- ◆ **Come to agreement on a schoolwide handwriting policy**.

  - Get together first by grade levels and then across grade levels. Spell out expectations and guidelines for when, what, and how to teach letter formation in manuscript or cursive writing, the appropriate writing paper to be used by each grade level, and if a formal program needs to be incorporated.

  - Don't go overboard! Ten minutes a day of "formal" handwriting instruction is probably sufficient until students have solid letter formation. Also, take the opportunity to teach on the spot when students incorrectly form letters in everyday writing and when we confer with them.

- ◆ **Value handwritten pieces**. Call me old-fashioned, but I still love to receive a handwritten note and prefer it to a greeting card with a predetermined message. Special handwritten notes to friends and colleagues and condolence letters benefit from the personal touch by the writer, not just the handwriting but also the selected paper that is used.

  - Ensure that at least some of students' published work that is shared, distributed, and posted is handwritten.

  - Make exceptions for those students physically unable to legibly write by hand. Make accommodations with a computer or other device.

Collaborate more

When I first began teaching, most of my time was behind closed doors with my students. I have few memories of coteaching, coaching, or working with colleagues. It was pretty much a "lone wolf" culture, and part of me preferred that. I could "hide out." My mistakes or failed lessons would not become public knowledge, and I didn't have to take many risks. If I'm an effective teacher today, it's largely because of what I've learned with and from others—through professional reading, professional conversations, observing experts, seeking feedback—and, especially, through ongoing collaboration with colleagues. In fact, in all schools that are high achieving, professional collaboration and trust permeate the culture and day-to-day relationships of the school. Meaningful collaboration and the ability to work well with others are attributes of workers in highly successful organizations of all types.

Take action

- **Seek to establish ongoing and high-level professional development** at our schools, even if we have to start the process ourselves with just a few colleagues (see p. 133).

- **Admit what we don't know** and seek out, observe, and have a dialogue with more knowledgeable peers. Ask a trusted peer to review a lesson plan, give feedback on a lesson, or coteach.

- **Be open to coaching**. Positive coaching experiences have the potential to vastly improve our teaching (see "Put a Whole-School Plan Into Practice" in *Teaching Essentials*, Routman, 2008a, pp. 116–124).

- **Work with the principal** to schedule times for common planning with grade levels or content area teachers, peer observations, and peer coaching.

- **Establish a school-based leadership team**, led by the principal, with representatives from each grade level and key disciplines to plan and carry out the school's ongoing professional development (see www.regieroutman.com/inresidence/default.aspx, which has been designed for that purpose).

Slow down to hurry up

Every time I move students too quickly to application, disaster strikes. Instead of a classroom full of students who know exactly what is expected and how "to do it," I wind up with many poorly done writing papers or too many students unable to deeply comprehend the reading text. Here's what I'm talking about. In a recent writing residency, where I was demonstrating and coaching teachers in conferring, the conferences were exhausting! Most of the students' drafts needed major reorganization work because I hadn't done enough frontloading (p. 73) and set out clear enough expectations. The end result was that I had more work to do with lots of reteaching and rethinking. Not only was it all frustrating and time consuming, but also I lost students' initial enthusiasm for the writing work.

It takes courage and a shift in beliefs to slow down and teach for depth. One teacher told me that initially she didn't believe that teaching less, but teaching more thoroughly, would pay off. It took until the middle of the school year for her to see that her students were actually much further along as readers and writers. Not only that, the number of students needing intervention had significantly decreased.

Use simple rubrics

One surefire way to ensure students know exactly what to do and how to do it is to create a simple rubric with them that specifically lists the required criteria, *after* we have shown them exactly what they are expected to do. For example, in a combined second- and third-grade class where we were writing unlikely friendship stories (see p. 58) which would become a class book, I thought aloud as I wrote my story in front of the class and then we created a simple three-part rubric based on what I had included: What happened? What was the kindness? What was the lesson learned? After we had done sufficient frontloading (see p. 73), each student completed a draft within 30 minutes. All 23 students were successful! Everyone included a satisfying lead, elaboration on the kindness that changed their thinking, and a closure that delineated the lesson learned. The biggest advantage was the pride every student felt at having been successful. The conferences were joyful and gave energy, rather than taking it away! Another huge advantage was that because there was little revision to do, students were willing to assume responsibility for the hard work of editing. Having a clear and easy-to-follow rubric is often key to classwide writing success on first drafts.

Take action

- **Create clear guidelines**. Make sure the language and directions can be easily understood and followed by students. Sometimes we complicate activities by making rubrics too complex, for example, by writing them in adult language or using rubrics written by publishers.

- **Expect students to self-evaluate**. Do not confer with students until they have shown us they have met all the criteria on the agreed-upon rubric (for solving a problem, conducting research, reading, editing, and so on).

- **Be judicious in the use of rubrics**. We don't need rubrics for every activity and piece of writing. Eventually we want students to internalize, for example, what good writers and researchers do, without the need for a rubric.

Expect change

I'll never forget how physically uncomfortable I was when, in our first year of marriage, Frank, my architect-husband, regularly rearranged our living room in more ways than I thought possible. I was used to room stability—that is, once a sofa and tables were in a spot where they looked good, they stayed there for at least 10 years! It's easy to do the same thing with our teaching. We believe things are working as well as possible, so why change them? Here's what I've learned: Not only did I eventually come to embrace changes in our home, I began initiating them because I learned to see fresh possibilities I couldn't have previously imagined. It took years but, today, I welcome change and see it as a necessity to thrive. That's not to say I find it easy. While established routines and lessons provide important structure and comfort, worthwhile change invigorates us and expands our thinking and actions beyond what we believed was attainable. A school story comes to mind.

On the first day of a residency in a school, where most students were from low-income families and were achieving two years below grade level, many teachers were sitting warily with arms folded. After warm introductions and optimistic talk about what could be possible (with the principal's prior permission), I said to them: "If you're not willing to go on this journey of change with us, you may want to consider teaching in another school. I don't mean to offend you, but this is not about you; our work together is about doing right by our students, and they deserve the best we can offer them." After two years of ongoing professional development centered around effective literacy practices, no teachers had chosen to leave, literacy achievement was clearly on the rise—as evidenced by district and state evaluations and tests—and the culture of the school had become collaborative and positive. In fact, some teachers from other schools applied to teach at the school because it became a hub of energy and optimism for what *all* students could achieve.

Change is a constant and a necessary fact of life. While we do need to resist harmful change and change as an end in itself, we must adjust our practices to encompass current thinking and experiences, new learning, and valid research. Being open to change is the sign of a healthy organization, and while change itself does not guarantee improvement, thoughtfully planned change can work to serve our students and us better and more equitably. Not only that, but when change leads us to become more knowledgeable and effective as educators, we feel rejuvenated, energetic, and joyful. The bottom line is to expect change, involve everyone, and accept the fact that lasting change takes time.

Apply whole-part-whole teaching

It's counterintuitive. We would think that it's easier and more manageable for students, especially our struggling ones, if we break texts and activities up into little parts. Actually, we make it much harder for students to successfully learn. A colleague put it this way: It's like putting all the pieces of a big puzzle in front of someone but never showing him or her the lid of the box. Starting with the whole of a meaningful text, context, story, or activity is always easier for the brain to make sense of and makes success more likely, even for our youngest learners, as the following story illustrates.

I was working in a high-needs kindergarten classroom in March of the school year where students had been reading and writing for authentic audiences and purposes since the beginning of the school year. The teacher and I were having the students write "how to" directions that would be posted in the classroom and around the school. We wrote "How to Line Up" together, as a shared writing, brainstormed many "how to" topics they could choose from, and had several public, scaffolded conversations with students before sending them off to write. We directed them to write only the first line, their lead, for two reasons: (1) We wanted to ensure they understood how to begin so they, and we, wouldn't have to redo and (2) We didn't want to overwhelm them. To our surprise and chagrin, all students got down a meaningful first sentence, and more than half of them wrote the entire "How to" text in one sitting! What a big learning experience that was. It was actually easier for most of them to write three to five sentences and keep the flow of writing going than to stop after one beginning thought. Our meager expectations limited their capacity but, luckily, most of them ignored us.

Take action

- **Tell the whole story first**, even if we only write a small part of it. This advice applies to us and to our students. Telling the whole story first encourages the use of elaboration and detail and helps us flesh out what's most important. Starting with oral storytelling, with guided support, also makes it easier for most learners to tell and write a complete story.

- **Provide some context**. When assessing comprehension through one-on-one reading conferences, have students bring a book-in-process or a completed book. Sometimes, the reader needs to have read at least several pages before full meaning kicks in. Having some idea of the content and how the text works before an assessment makes deeper comprehension more likely.

- ◆ **Rethink exercises in isolation**. There is no research that shows that isolated skills work helps kids learn more or faster. Embed explicit skills teaching and practice within the context of the meaningful content we are teaching. Keep in mind that every well-written text contains multiple opportunities for teaching vocabulary, word work, writing craft, and reading comprehension.

Live an interesting life

Years ago I was in danger of becoming a very boring person. Most of my time outside of work was spent reading and studying educational issues. I was not a fascinating conversationalist at parties. I could not talk smartly about history, world issues, or great literature. My husband, who is an artist, encouraged me to expand my narrow horizons. How we live our lives outside of school matters. When we have interesting stories to tell and new ideas to share, we enter our school and classroom with a sense of rejuvenation. If we spend most of our evenings and weekends on time-consuming lesson plans, elaborate projects, and grading papers, we come into school without the energy and spark to energize our students and peers. Make time for reading for pleasure, exercising with a friend, gardening, dancing, cooking a special meal, walking, visiting with loved ones, learning about a topic outside of education, or whatever brings us pleasure and satisfaction. Remember, there is no research that shows that those of us who spend the most hours planning lessons and marking papers have the highest student achievement. An evening spent attending a marvelous theater performance, creating a splendid meal, dining with friends, listening to classical music or jazz, or reading terrific nonfiction or fiction gives me energy to teach.

See www.regieroutman.org for my blog posts, which include short, personal essays on how my life experiences have an impact on and intersect with my teaching.

Put the language in their ears

Teachers are often surprised when I explicitly suggest language possibilities to students, but putting the language in their ears is smart teaching that pays big dividends. That is, the quality of the work the student produces is higher than when we leave all the thinking work to the student. Primarily, we use what I call scaffolded conversations, and many of these are done publicly at the front of the class, with one student or a small group, with the whole class looking on. In that way, all students benefit and get ideas for their own writing or literature discussion of a book or curriculum topic.

In a scaffolded conversation, the child verbalizes his ideas on a topic the teacher has already demonstrated through her own writing or leading of a discussion. Through back and forth conversation and guided questioning, we encourage and prompt the student to clarify and elaborate in a meaningful and engaging manner. We also suggest language the child might want to try out. Scaffolded conversations are an essential part of the "we do it" in the Optimal Learning Model (p. 15). These supported conversations are crucial to the success of English-language learners, students who struggle, and to those who lack the confidence, know-how, and practice to speak and write connected and interesting thoughts on their own.

Take action

♦ **Suggest specific language to the student**. There is no script here, and it's not just "Tell me more." Imagine that we are having a conversation with a fascinating individual. What do we want to know? How can we help that person tell his story or express his thoughts more fully? We might say something like,

- "What did you say to your dad after that happened? Did you say something like, 'Dad, how you could you do that?' 'Or, did you say...'" (to promote the use of dialogue and in-the-moment writing)

- "What were you thinking? Just put us back in that moment when... How did you feel? Were you surprised, scared, or worried?" (to slow down the writing and encourage elaboration and detail)

- "Let's go back to the text. Where does the author say that? Let's look at page.... Here the author says...but I'm thinking that means...because of

104

the previous paragraph..." (to promote the use of close reading before analyzing an author's message.)

- **Help the student recall unique language**. We want the student to use the interesting words and phrases that emerge orally in the scaffolded conversation—in their writing and speaking. So that the student and we can recall the actual language, write those words on a sticky note and give it to the student to affix to his writing. In that way, we let the student know that we value the unique language and encourage its use. We, also, have now preserved that language for reference when we confer with the student.

- **Go deep, and take our time**. Hold fewer scaffolded conversations, but make them worthwhile. Two in-depth conversations will teach students more than many quick ones that skim the surface.

Aim for seamless teaching

A teacher lamented that she had lost the "flow" of her teaching. On some days her lessons still moved along well, but mostly she felt frustrated: "The new standards are raising expectations but fragmenting teaching." Or, again, a group of teachers complained they felt bound by a rigid structure. Required programs that once seemed like a supportive framework were now constraining teaching, and teachers worried that neither they nor their students were enjoying reading or writing much. They didn't know how to move forward. As one teacher put it, "We have all the pieces but don't know what to do with them."

Seamless teaching involves flow. Flow is an intensely pleasurable cognitive and physical state in which we are mindfully and optimally focused, involved, and motivated by the task or experience at hand. We become so caught up and unselfconscious in what we are doing that we lose track of everything else but the task at hand. Flow has been best described and researched by Russian psychologist, Mihaly Csikszentmihalyi, since the 1960s, when he sought to discover how some artists became so immersed in their work that they disregarded everything else going on around them. (You can hear and see Csikszentmihalyi on YouTube; presentation at the February 2004 TED conference.).

I recently observed a teacher in a state of flow. She was teaching poetry writing to her classroom of fetal alcohol syndrome students, and she and her students were completely absorbed in deep concentration of rereading and revising the poem they were writing. Seamlessly, she asked questions, sought interaction, and gave feedback that respected and stretched students' engagement, thinking, and responses. She had been teaching for about 20 years, and she was masterful.

Seamless teaching looks easy and natural when we see it, but acquiring that "ease" generally takes years of reflection, self-evaluation, and astute professional knowledge of knowing the questions to ask and when to ask them, the language and feedback that will move learning forward, and how and when to pose just enough of a challenge to successfully engage and enliven all learners. When our teaching is seamless, we are able to purposefully and intelligently think and act, moment-to-moment, in the act of teaching, as we responsively and responsibly assess, adjust, and innovate in order to achieve more and enjoy our work more fully. Flow is not just a goal for our teaching, learning, and leading but also for interacting and working more effectively with our colleagues and for living our lives more fully.

Nurture vocabulary development

It's essential that we expand vocabulary development for all students. For the most part, students who do well in school have a large vocabulary of words they understand and apply. Not only is a rich vocabulary a necessity for understanding and creating meaningful texts, but also it's fun to talk about and use words in various ways. Kids are naturally curious about words and word play, what words mean, and how words work, generally and specifically. In addition, students who own a rich storehouse of words tend to be higher achievers, and most of these students are avid readers. For our English-language learners and students who struggle, understanding and applying key vocabulary words are vital. It is often a lack of academic vocabulary that severely limits students' understanding of content and concepts.

Take action

◆ **Make a daily commitment to vocabulary development**:

- Provide explicit vocabulary instruction. Important keywords and definitions must be directly taught in order for students to grasp their meaning(s). Use explanations, demonstrations of use, physical involvement, prior knowledge, and as many senses as possible to make word meanings comprehensible.

- Advocate for extensive reading. Many words used in literature and informational pieces are not ordinarily part of everyday spoken language, so the only way to learn them is through extensive reading in a wide variety of genres.

- Connect independent reading time to vocabulary growth. On occasion, ask students to pick out and talk about one or two new words for which they figured out the meaning.

- Make it smart to ask about interesting words for which we don't know the meaning. For example, we can say, "Thomas asked what *solution* means. That's what successful learners do so they can understand more."

- Point out interesting words and how they are used when reading aloud to the class. Check with a librarian for more books like *Miss Alaineus: A Vocabulary Disaster* by Debra Frasier and *Donovan's Word Jar* by Monalisa DeGross that make vocabulary work fun and engrossing.

♦ **Develop a word-conscious classroom**.

- Notice and talk about interesting words wherever they turn up, demonstrate their use and meanings, and find opportunities to use keywords over and over again—in speaking and writing.

- Encourage students to try out the use of special focus words throughout the day, through our modeling and with our support, in conversations and in writing.

- Use word walls in the content areas—science, social studies, math, music, and so on—with definitions of significant words written with students.

- Feature a "vocabulary word of the day," with an explanation students can understand. Some days we can choose the word; other days a student chooses. These unique words and their meaning can be compiled into a Classroom Vocabulary Notebook.

Rely on shared writing

Regardless of the grade or content area we teaching, depending on shared writing is one of the most effective and efficient ways to ensure literacy success for all students. In shared writing, the teacher "holds the pen" and does the actual transcription while leading, guiding, accepting, and shaping student thinking. Shared writing makes it possible to raise expectations, show what's possible, and provide opportunities for all students to contribute their thoughts and ideas, without fear of failure. Often done whole class, shared writing—when conducted in an atmosphere of trust and respect—makes all students feel validated and successful. For complete, detailed information on shared writing, see *Writing Essentials* (Routman, 2005).

Take action

- **Accept all students' ideas**. Even if a student is off track, try to validate some part of the student's thinking. We want to affirm students for taking risks, and we want to honor their thinking. We can say something like, "Say more about that." Or, "How about if we say it like this...?" Or, "Let me come back to you again in a few minutes...listen to a few more ideas, and I'll help you..."

- **Encourage all students' voices to be heard**:

  - Call on a student who does not normally speak and say something like, "Valerie, your thinking is important, too. Which idea do you like best so far? Can you read that one (on the chart) out loud? Do you want to add anything?"

  - Put students into small, heterogeneous groups to revise the shared writing draft, give a word-processed copy to each group and appoint a scribe, and use the revised draft, signed by all group members, as an assessment of students' thinking and collaborative work. Bring the whole class back together and have each group contribute its ideas to a final draft that we help shape.

- **Turn shared writing texts into shared reading texts**. Because the texts are in students' own language, these are easy and engaging for students to read. Not only that, but all the word work students need—especially in the early grades—can come from these authentic contexts, which makes word study more enjoyable and far more efficient. Also, for second-language learners, creating shared writing texts as bilingual books offers much support to emerging readers.

- **Use shared writing texts to teach older students who struggle**. Write texts for reading—for, with, and by students—and word process the revised copies to be used for shared, partner, guided, or independent reading. Especially for students who have experienced years of failure and are turned off to school, meeting with a small group of reluctant readers and writing a text together on a topic they care passionately about, such as sports or video games, can be a turning point for long-struggling students becoming readers.

- **Create resources**. Use shared writing to create assessment charts, rubrics, research guidelines, procedures to follow, explanations—all in student-friendly language that make the charts accessible and useful. In addition, having a class book devoted to student-authored shared writing, to which we continue to add, provides lots of familiar reading and builds fluency and competence.

View celebration as teaching

Celebration is the heart and soul of my best teaching. I say that because every time we congratulate the learner on something done well, we affirm the behavior, skill, strategy, or effort and, therefore, make it more likely the learner will "do it again." This is as true for us as educators as it is for our students. Celebration is not just the actions we take or the words we use; it's a mindset and demeanor that propel us to primarily see, observe, and value strengths. By celebration, I mean noticing and commenting on everything the learner does well. In a reading conference, we comment on the learner's strengths—for example, choosing a "just right" book, figuring out vocabulary, getting the gist of the story—before we move to one or two teaching needs. In a writing content conference, we comment specifically on the language the learner has used to engage and sustain the reader's interest, for example, by reading aloud the actual beginning lead with the language and style that hooks the reader. If it's a public conference, we let observing students know that "one of the reasons we're having a public conference is so that you can learn from all the terrific things another student has done and apply them to your own writing." In fact, our explicit celebrations of one student become teaching points for all students.

Perhaps what I love best about celebration is its power to change and elevate a life, in and out of school. Especially in writing, I have literally seen students, who envision themselves as struggling, change before our eyes after they have been well celebrated. Not only that, but their standing among their peers improves, and the culture of the classroom is enriched and improved. Peers who previously thought, "He can't do that very well" or "He's not very smart" are now beginning to shift to, "I didn't know he could do that. He knows more than I thought." With that shift comes a more positive stance towards the student and a stronger community of learners.

Establish a rich and relevant classroom library

For one of my first teaching residencies, I was invited to a school to raise reading achievement and test scores. It was a typical school, just outside a large urban area, where the teachers believed they were doing everything they could as teachers of reading and, yet, achievement—based on test scores—was stagnant. It took only one day to figure out the problem. Not only were students not reading much or enjoying reading, but also there were no classroom libraries, no teaching for deep comprehension, and there was an overreliance on a core reading program. Our focus for the entire first year was on creating beautiful and accessible classroom libraries with student input, teaching students how to self-select "just-right" books in various genres, setting up a daily, carefully monitored independent reading program, and relying on reading-on as our primary follow-up work to guided reading groups. For the second year, with the libraries as the mainstay of daily reading in every classroom, we moved our focus to guided reading, but it was guided reading as a means to facilitate students' being able to read and self-monitor on their own, not as an end in itself.

Take action

- **Make our classroom library the centerpiece of our classroom**. Enter the classroom with fresh eyes. Look closely to make sure the library corner is prominent, attractive, well organized, and has book covers facing out, as much as possible, for easy browsing and accessibility. Also, where possible, include an adjacent floor area or designated space where students can read comfortably.

- **Involve students in setting up and maintaining the library**. Start the collection, if need be, by borrowing a large number of books from the school and public library and, if possible, securing loans from students' home collections too. Include a variety of series, predictable and patterned books, informational books, poetry, texts by favorite authors including student authors, many genres including graphic novels, and whatever kinds of texts interest our students. Balance the collection with at least 50% nonfiction. If books are in bins, have students handwrite the labels for the categories for the bins, to create a personalized look. Be sure the library is organized with students so there is joint ownership, which increases usage and enjoyment.

- ◆ **Be cautious about leveling books**. Just as we would not expect to be directed to a particular level in the public library, think about grouping books by categories, rather than levels, and explicitly teaching students how to select books they can read and understand. Leveled texts are fine for guided reading and for students still struggling to choose books they can read but, for most of us, having a wide range of choices works best.

- ◆ **Connect reading conferences to independent reading**. Because almost all reading is done silently and independently, provide daily, sustained reading practice time on self-selected books, and confer one-on-one with students to celebrate their strengths, ensure they comprehend deeply, and to determine teaching needs.

Reduce the need for intervention

It happens so often that I see it as a major concern. In the course of planning for a residency, when I ask the principal and teachers about pressing literacy needs, the first thing that often comes up is how to deal with difficult student behaviors. As a typical example, in a school where most of the students are from low-income families and are receiving free and reduced-cost meals, I learn that as much as a quarter of the students are on medications for various reasons—hyperactivity, post-traumatic stress, depression, and more. Some of these students are apparently unable to function without an aide, who has been assigned to them. As always, I insist all students be present for the residency and that I don't want to know anyone's label. And, as always, by week's end every student is fully participating, and it's impossible to pick out the labeled ones. I've come to believe we are overidentifying students with special needs, and that when we provide a relevant and engaging curriculum, teach with a sense of urgency and joy, respectfully invite everyone into the conversations, and celebrate strengths and small victories, weaknesses and behavioral problems can disappear.

As well, when we offer excellent first teaching to all students and put our literacy efforts at the universal level (see "Ensure excellent first instruction for *all* students," p. 117) we effectively reduce our special education population. In one such elementary school that moved to intervention as a last resort, the number of students receiving special education services went from 18% to 3% over a three-year period, saving the school more than $100,000 per year, as the services of two full-time, special education teachers were no longer required.

Take a close look at the number of students we are identifying as requiring intervention. When the percentages are high, and most of our identified students qualify for free and reduced-cost meals, are African American or Hispanic, or are English-language learners, we need to pause, reflect, and ask the hard question: Are we resorting to intervention before offering all students an opportunity to experience and engage in the same excellent instruction we offer our gifted students? An equitable literacy focus requires ongoing, embedded professional development across a whole school (see p. 133), a mind-set that believes in focusing on the universal level first, and our collaborative advocacy for first-rate reading and writing instruction for all.

Tell the truth

I never lie to students. I am careful with the language I use, but whether the student is a struggling reader or writer or a gifted one, we deal with matters honestly and tactfully. Our students and their families have the right to know the achievement realities and possibilities. If we are caring, transparent, and authentic in our motives, honesty really is the best policy. What follows are two brief stories where telling the truth led students to assume more responsibility for higher achievement and deeper understanding.

Robert was a confident, gifted sixth grader who was finishing lengthy and complex chapter books at an amazing pace. When I sat down with him for a one-on-one reading conference and took the time to assess for deep understanding, I learned that his reading was shallow—that is, he could talk about plot but had only superficial understanding of a book's major themes or why characters behave as they do and the consequences of their actions. I told him, "Robert, you are a very strong reader, you seem to like reading, and you read a lot, which is great. But you read so fast that you are missing a lot of what's most important in the book. In our conference, I never saw you go back and reread to clarify meaning or figure out vocabulary. In talking about the book, you were not able to talk much about the main character's motivation. You're a straight A student, and your test scores are high, so no one will ever know if you keep on reading book after book as you are doing now. But you will know. And you will know you can do better. It's up to you. You can either continue along with your rapid-fire reading or slow down and read for deep understanding, which will, ultimately, also increase your enjoyment. It's your choice."

When I saw Robert again, several months later, he had taken to heart the importance and joy of slower reading for greater meaning. With a huge smile he told me, "I'm loving reading now, and I'm taking my time. And I'm learning and understanding a whole lot more."

Jordan was a fourth grader cruising though levels and reading two years below grade level. Neither she nor her teacher were holding her accountable for being a better reader, and Jordan seemed unaware of how far behind she was. In a one-on-one reading conference, where it became clear that she was far more capable than her lackluster efforts indicated, I said something like, "Jordan, I can tell from our conference that you're not reading much at home or in school. By the fact that you read so slowly and finish very few books, it's not likely you're going to become a great reader. I can also tell you understand what you read, so that's great. But right now, you're just reading easy books that are at about a second-grade level and you're in fourth grade. If you want to do well in school and accomplish your dreams, you need to push yourself a lot harder, starting now. You need to do a lot more reading, and you need to challenge yourself more."

Back at her school a year later, Jordan, who was now a fifth grader, tracked me down and insisted on meeting with me. Here's part of what she proudly told me: "When you told me I was two years below where I should be, I was shocked! I couldn't believe it, so I started working harder and reading more. I read every night now, and my reading is a lot better." Jordan, through her own efforts and with her teacher's support, was now reading and understanding texts at her grade level.

Ensure excellent first instruction for *all* students

Put most of our efforts into universal, exemplary instruction for all students. We can substantially reduce the number of students who need intervention when good first teaching is the norm. When I work in a school, I insist that all students, even those who would ordinarily not be in the classroom at that time, be included. Amazing things can and do happen. With support, students can and do achieve at levels that we, and they, did not know was possible. Kathy is one such student. Now a college sophomore, as a fifth grader who was a second-language learner and special education student, she was included in a reading residency (without my knowing her labels) where she would normally have been excluded. Given the opportunity to participate in listening to a complex text—followed by high-level discussion—she took it all in, although she was initially silent. An in-depth reading conference confirmed that a lack of decoding skills was impeding her overall achievement. With intensive, once-a-week phonics instruction and extensive reading of books at her "just right" level, she was reading on grade level within several months. Two years later, through her own advocacy efforts, she finally succeeded in removing her special education classification (see bottom of p. 40 for her story).

Take action

- **Assume all students are intelligent**. Through our body language, tone of voice, choice of words, willingness to be supportive, and explicit and purposeful instruction, we can convey "you can do it" to every student.

- **Advocate for practices and resources that serve all students well**. For example, rely on first-rate texts and primary sources, not just published core programs. Also, study the research and results behind new program adoptions before a purchase is made. When the program seems inappropriate for the student body, join with our colleagues to get involved, ask pertinent questions, speak up, and suggest alternatives.

- **Work to make sure that a school's and district's policies and master schedule do not disadvantage students**, for example, pulling students out for support during a rich language arts class. Endeavor to establish practices and schedules that keep students' needs primary, not the educational specialist's.

- **Consider not reading students' files before they enter our classrooms**. That makes it more likely for us to see all students as capable of learning at high levels.

Make students less dependent on us

A kind and caring intermediate grades teacher complained that her students were always seeking her attention and help. It was getting harder to meet with small groups and to confer with students one-on-one. In fact, she had a long line of students at her desk on most days, especially during writing time. I suggested she emphatically tell her students that they could no longer seek her out while she was with another student or group and that from now on they would be expected to find misspellings, use resources, and do everything she had taught them how to do before she would agree to help them. She told the whole staff, "It was like a miracle. I didn't really believe it would work, but it did! I sternly told the kids, 'You can no longer approach me when I'm working with students. Find the help you need. You can quietly ask a friend, you can try everything you know, but you cannot come to me.' Amazingly, the room got quiet, everyone was working, and I could finally do my job. What a revelation!"

Take action

- **State clear and reasonable expectations** for students and expect them to meet them. We do need, first, to demonstrate exactly what those expectations look like and sound like in practice. Although initially it can take longer not to "fix" everything ourselves, it's a win–win situation in the long run— less work for us, and more responsibility and independence for our students, which is more productive and satisfying all around.

- **Teach self-checking**. Rather than having us check all answers and papers, set up systems where students can self-evaluate, self-monitor, and self-correct— beginning in kindergarten (see p. 51 for an example).

- **Have useful resources available and accessible**, and teach students how to use them. For example, word walls, anchor charts, posted directions, student-friendly spelling resources, and former students' work to be used as exemplars

- **Set up routines and rituals** with students, and hold them accountable for ensuring those activities go as they have been set up, including procedures and solutions for dealing with problems (see p. 94).

- **Rely on more partner and small group work**. Once we have applied an Optimal Learning Model to our instruction and students know how and what to do, peers can effectively help each other with spelling, reading, conferring, and much more.

Establish routines and rituals

Daily routines ground me and enable me to approach the tasks of the day with a sense of stability and optimism. For example, my husband Frank and I enjoy a breakfast ritual, which provides a tranquil start to our day. Frank cooks a full breakfast of eggs, pancakes, or oatmeal with all the trimmings, but not before handing me a steaming cup of Seattle's finest, coffee made with just-ground, locally roasted beans topped with hot, hand foamed, low-fat milk. He knows that I appreciate the indulgence and that I can barely speak or function without that morning brew. Then, over a delicious and leisurely breakfast, I read *The New York Times* (the actual paper version) while he reads *The Seattle Times*. We do have some conversation about the news and politics but, mostly, it's a peaceful, unhurried time that fortifies me with the energy, calm, and resolve to begin the messy, hard work of writing each day.

I believe routines and rituals also give our students a sense of calm and stability, knowing there are predictable things they can count on, whether it's the way we greet them in the morning or the way students collaborate in small groups. Knowing what to expect creates an order and comfort that makes it easier for students—and us, as well—to positively respond to the inevitable changes that occur in the unpredictable life of the classroom and school. Daily routines also help build stamina (see p. 147).

Take action

◆ **Develop daily routines and rituals with our students**. A routine or ritual may be as simple as students having reading choices before school officially begins or as complex as knowing how to self-direct a literature conversation group. Some daily routines and rituals might include, but are not limited to:

- Establishing procedures for how the classroom operates—jobs, bathroom use, solutions for problem solving classroom issues that arise, recess rules and permitted games, guidelines for substitutes and visitors.

- Maintaining the classroom library with students—sign out, organization, book return, adding new texts and categories.

- Coming to agreement on before-school and end-of-day activities.

◆ **Create predictable structures**

- Try to schedule writing at the same time every day, so students come depend on it, anticipate it, and are ready to write. Especially for our youngest students, think about scheduling writing in the morning when their energy and concentration are highest.

- Examine daily schedules and work with the principal, grade level, and specialists to ensure key subject areas times are not fragmented, which causes students to lose concentration and time on task.

- Work to minimize pull outs and to ensure all students are present for rich literacy and language activities.

◆ **Include celebration** as part of the daily life of the classroom. Develop rituals for birthdays, special occasions, notable accomplishments, hard-fought efforts, and so on.

Be a leader as well as a team member

One of my greatest learning lessons in the whole-school change process has been this one: Principals have to know literacy, and teachers need to be leaders. I used to think that if principals were strong leaders and teachers were excellent at instruction, high student achievement would result. Certainly that has been true for some teachers and some students. But for sustainable change, we need a whole school of highly knowledgeable, highly achieving teachers and students. That requires all teachers to assume a leadership role and for principals to assume a major literacy role. I define a leader as someone who recognizes what needs to be done for the good of the organization, initiates ideas, welcomes and seeks others' input and suggestions and, who then takes appropriate action to help guide the organization to move forward in a respectful and collaborative manner.

Take action

- **Share promising ideas with our principal and colleagues**. Distribute copies of excellent professional articles, important news of the profession, and timely research.

- **Become a team leader**. Ensure that each grade level meets regularly to plan together, exchange ideas, and support each other. If no such team exists, start one and offer to facilitate the meetings. Request that another member take notes of the meetings and copy those for the team and the principal.

- **Take the lead on schoolwide professional development**. Even if we start with a small group of volunteers, begin to meet regularly to focus on improved instruction and learning. Go beyond looking at and analyzing data to observing, discussing, and applying—with collegial support—best practices to the classroom.

- **Form a school leadership team** with the principal and representation by grade levels in order to plan, organize, and carry out ongoing professional development based on staff and student needs, data analysis, and agreed upon literacy goals (see p. 97).

Esteem every learner

When our son Peter was in fifth grade, he had his best teacher. By "best," I mean she was the first teacher who saw and valued our son as a unique individual with special talents. During parent–teacher conference time, she talked about Peter's kindness, curiosity, and ability to get along well with everyone. She told stories to illustrate those admirable traits. She did not focus first on a messy desk or occasional late homework, as a former teacher had done. In fact, I only remember the constant smile on her face and the steady stream of celebratory comments as she talked about "our boy, Pete." Peter blossomed that year—and not just academically. With an August birthday, he was one of the youngest students in his class and, previously, had been a bit shy. Not that year. He became a class leader and a voracious reader, and he soared academically. Today, he has no recollection of what he learned academically; what he vividly remembers is, "She believed in me." At the end of the school year, my husband Frank and I sent his teacher a dozen red roses as a thank you. She won our hearts because she understood and admired our son and helped him realize his full potential. Peter and I still talk about his extraordinary fifth grade teacher and her lasting influence on him. Her name was Marty Singleton.

So many times, I've seen a student make a leap as a reader and writer once that student feels intrinsically valued. It's no less true for us educators. Many of us feel we don't measure up. It's no surprise really with the unrelenting pressure to raise achievement in what is already a high-demand teaching and learning environment. It's a wise principal and a staff-as-cohesive community who act upon the knowledge that we teachers first need recognition and understanding for what we are doing well—and attempting to do—as teacher–learners. Only then do we have the energy and positive mind-set needed to maximize our instruction for improved student learning.

Use common sense

Often, at the end of a residency, teachers will say, "So much of what you do is common sense." Well, yes, it is. When did we go so far afield that we think nothing of doing things that make no sense! If something sounds too good to be true, it probably is. Being able to apply common sense depends on deep knowledge of literacy and learning as well as a firm foundation of beliefs that match best practices. Common sense in teaching is not based on blind intuition or a gut feel; it is knowing how to act in a sensible manner based on reason, experience, data, and the students in front of us. Applying common sense requires competence, confidence, and a strong desire to do right by our students.

Take action

- **Use resources judiciously**. Rather than following a program or resource lock-step, employ that program as a framework. Choose and use what matches our curriculum, standards, beliefs, practices, and students' needs and interests. Don't be afraid to change the order of recommended activities or texts so they make more sense or to skip and set aside activities, worksheets, and texts that aren't relevant, appropriate, or worth our time.

- **Do not overrely on core reading programs**. The most comprehensive analysis of the major core reading programs conclusively shows, among other findings, that such programs do not adequately teach comprehension, teach too many skills and strategies, move too quickly from one skill or strategy to the next without sufficient practice time, and disadvantage readers who struggle by expecting them to read texts that are too difficult (Dewitz, Jones, & Leahy, 2009). Therefore, it becomes a necessity for us teachers to fill in the holes and know how to teach reading comprehension in depth.

- **Follow our knowledgeable instincts**, but first gather as much data and information as we can. Remember, there is no one best way to teach or assess, and when someone tells us that there is, we need to question it and apply common sense.

- **Advocate for saner practices**. Applying common sense takes courage. We must speak up and advocate for what we believe. For example, if our schools and districts are pressuring us to act in ways that are harmful to students or that disadvantage them, we have a moral responsibility to make our voices heard and to suggest and lobby for alternative, beneficial approaches.

Do more shared reading

Shared reading is ideal for building fluency, automaticity, stamina, reading skills and strategies, and enjoyment for learners of all ages. In shared reading, we teachers (or another expert) provide an engaging text to every reader—either through individual copies, an enlarged copy such as a "big book," or a projected copy that all can see—and invite everyone to read along. (Notice where shared reading fits in the Optimal Learning Model, see p. 15). Our reading demonstrations and support, as we read the text together, give students the competence and confidence to eventually read and understand the text on their own. Sometimes the text is a familiar one, created through shared writing. Other times, it's an unfamiliar one that we have determined most of the students will be able to read, with our support.

Take action

- **Be sure students know the purpose**. Before shared reading, say something like, "The reason we're reading this text together is so you can become a better reader, so make sure your eyes are on the text, even if you can't read every word." Or, "We're going to read this text together and, then notice and learn together how the author helps us figure out difficult words in the passage. Then, when you're reading on your own, you'll know how to do that."

- **Read and enjoy the text as a whole first** before stopping to do word work and other analysis (see "Apply whole-part-whole teaching," p. 101).

- **Assess as we go**. Have another student come to the front of the classroom to lead a second or third reading so we can observe all students and intervene with students who are not on task. Stop and ask questions to check for understanding.

- **Use shared reading with older and younger readers**. Use narrative and informational picture books as well as a chapter or portion from a fiction or nonfiction text, including content area texts.

- **Employ shared reading aloud**—that is, combine reading aloud with shared reading and interactive reading. For example, after demonstrating such strategies as summarizing, predicting, inferring, and figuring out vocabulary in a text we have been reading aloud, choose a paragraph or page that almost all students can read and have them read and analyze it with us. Then, have students "try out," first in a small group or with a partner, reading a portion and applying the targeted strategy or strategies. Revisit the text with students and have them confirm or disconfirm their responses. For example, we might say to a student, "Show me the line(s) in the text where it says...," or, "Let's read together the part where the author shows us..."

◆ **Encourage rereading**. Use partner reading, guided reading, and independent reading to have students practice the shared reading text for fluency and strategies we have been demonstrating.

For much more on shared reading and shared reading aloud, see *Reading Essentials* (Routman, 2003, pp. 130–149) and *Transforming Our Teaching Through Reading to Understand* (Routman, 2009).

Put energy where results are most likely

When I first started working as a literacy coach in schools, I was equitable about how I spent my time. I believed in trying to get every single teacher "on board" with our literacy vision. The same was true when I began doing teaching and coaching residencies. In fact, in my first residencies, the host teacher, in whose classroom I did demonstration teaching and coaching for observing teachers, was often a weak teacher. I initially had to spend so much time on management that I wasn't able to teach with a sense of urgency or demonstrate all I had planned. More important, the host teacher wasn't strong enough to move forward after the residency, on her own, let alone mentor others.

Here's what I've learned: We can exhaust ourselves trying to work with colleagues who for various reasons, are very slow to change. My husband Frank helped me shift my thinking. He said, "You know how we both love to eat pistachio nuts. Well, when you come across that nut that's hard to crack, you can either break your fingernails trying to crack it or set it aside and move on. There's a whole bowl waiting for you." Today, I ask the principal to place me with the strongest teachers or teachers demonstrating high potential. In that way, we can maximize our teaching and learning time and have an impact on more teachers on staff. I coach the host teachers to take on what they've learned and to share it with others—that is, to be agreeable to opening their classrooms to all willing colleagues, to coplan and coteach, and to become literacy leaders in their schools.

Along the same lines, we must use caution and common sense on how much time we put into learning how to use and apply new district-mandated programs, new standards, and resources. All the time and energy it takes to learn new techniques and approaches must be worth our investment and the students.' The new resources must align with our beliefs, practices, and curriculum and not the other way around.

With our students, of course, it's our responsibility to reach and teach every one. To get great results, we need first-rate resources, expert teaching skills, additional support, and more. We also need to acknowledge that there is no "quick fix" in making the transition to more effective practices and that, in fact, it can take several years to see full benefits (see "Focus on the essential ingredients," p. 84). Some needed support in accelerating literacy achievement can come from peers or students in upper grades, such as when an upper grade class partners weekly with a primary-grade class in reading. "Each one, teach one" is a great philosophy as long as the person doing the teaching is knowledgeable and able to work well with others. We have only so much time and energy, and we must apportion it wisely and where it does the most good. Not only that, but also staying positive and optimistic about our daily work is essential to our overall effectiveness and well-being.

Promote significant conversations

Although lots of talk goes on in our classrooms, we need to work to ensure that our conversations are worthwhile—that is, they promote debate, curiosity, and thoughtful questioning, help students see issues from different points of view, and lead to valuing multiple perspectives, even for our youngest students. Productive and collaborative talk helps clarify meaning, improves retention of information, shapes and improves thinking capacities, leads to deeper understanding, and results in more enduring learning. "Learning how to interact effectively with others may be the most important skill that students develop in school" (Hammond & Nessel, 2011, p. 89). Even as we facilitate conversations, we want students to be doing most of the talking. Our role is to stimulate, clarify, and moderate the conversations so students talk and learn from each other. I explain to students, "Scientists (researchers) have found out you learn more from talking with each other than from just listening to the teacher. So it's important you listen well to each other."

Take action

- **Demonstrate what a literate conversation sounds like** through viewing and analyzing quality content videos with two or more speakers, having students observe us discussing with a colleague or student(s) and naming and explaining what we say and why we say it, or setting up and facilitating a "fish bowl" conversation, with an inner circle of heterogeneously grouped students in a teacher-led, guided discussion and an outer circle of observing students who are noting and recording characteristics of effective speakers and listeners. (Writing down what students observe also serves as our assessment.)

- **Create more opportunities for productive talk and discussion**. Use "turn and talk" throughout the day. Stop often during a lesson, after about 10 minutes, where we are doing most of the talking and have students turn to a partner or two to three students to discuss what has been learned, raise a question, make a prediction, and so on. Use those times to assess what students are learning and where we need to adjust our instruction (see "Do more student-directed, small-group work," p. 156).

- **Have more literature conversations** and talk about books. Self-directed literature conversations are excellent for promoting student-guided talk about all kinds of texts (see "Literature Conversations" in *Conversations*, Routman, 2000, pp. 171–204).

- **See and teach deeper listening as a way towards deeper conversations** (see "Become an active listener," p. 34).

Develop shared beliefs

Perhaps, more than any other dynamic, positive and lasting change in a school accelerates and takes hold only when the principal and staff come together on commonly held beliefs. Coherence of beliefs is essential for raising achievement across a school, but this is no easy matter. When staff members first come together to examine and discuss their beliefs about reading and writing, it is not unusual to wind up with only one or two beliefs everyone holds in common. Especially in schools where competing new programs are introduced every year or so, and where commercial materials, district mandates, and outside experts dominate curriculum and instructional decisions, teachers often don't know what they believe.

Our beliefs drive our practices, in every aspect of our lives, so it's crucial that we can articulate our beliefs, align them with sensible and research-based practices, and act upon them in a way that increases achievement, engagement, and enjoyment for our students and us. Having a core of 6–10 commonly held beliefs, for both teaching reading and for teaching writing, is essential for actualizing a school's vision statement and journey to higher achievement.

Take action

- ◆ **Come to agreement on literacy beliefs**. In vertical teams (represented by various grade levels and specialties), get together as a staff several times a year and have respectful and productive discussion around beliefs about teaching and learning (See *Regie Routman in Residence: Transforming Our Teaching*, video-based literacy series, Session 3 for protocols and procedures, www.regieroutman.com/inresidence/default.aspx).

- ◆ **Notice what's posted on walls and in hallways**. We can often determine a school's collective beliefs by a walk through the school. As one savvy colleague told me, "The walls talk."

  - • Make sure messages and texts that are posted are relevant, readable, correct, and geared to real readers and writers and that posted work pieces are not just artifacts taking up wall space.

  - • Note the language and format of class charts and resources. Look for charts that use student-friendly language and that have been created with students based on curriculum study, class needs, and interests. Check that posted charts and information are not primarily commercially produced and written.

- **Develop and use a common language** for essential literacy terms, such as *revision, editing, scaffolded conversations, content conferences, editing conferences, shared writing, shared reading, demonstrating,* and so on. In order to improve our practices across a school and district, we need to be employing the same specific, useful language along with what to look for in each literacy context.

- **Work to ensure that beliefs determine selected resources** and not the other way around. Too often a school's resources and programs are purchased without rigorous discussion and group input. We need to first establish our common beliefs and then seek out the resources and programs that can best support those beliefs.

Make professional development our priority

Too few schools have been willing to make the commitment to high-level, ongoing, school-based, professional development. As a profession and as a nation, we have not yet figured out that core programs, outside experts, new resources, or upgraded standards will not, by themselves, improve and sustain achievement. So we continue to tread water and march in place, and not much changes for too many students over the long run. The achievement gap between rich and poor students is greater than ever, and the gap for students of color and second-language learners is immense as well, with disproportionate numbers being labeled as special education.

Yet the research is strong and uncontested: The most powerful way to guarantee high-quality professional development and accompanying higher achievement is to embed professional development into the daily life and culture of the school. Professional learning communities (PLCs), focused on raising student literacy achievement across the curriculum, are a necessity. To be effective, professional development must be ongoing, composed of at least 30–100 hours of time over the school year, connected to classroom practice, and geared to fostering collegial collaboration (Darling-Hammond & Richardson, 2009; Guskey & Suk Yoon, 2009). Without a strong foundation of knowledge, we cannot effectively reflect upon and improve our practices. Participating in literacy-based PLCs is one of the best ways to become a highly effective and informed educator. Even if we are in a school or district with inadequate professional development, there is still much we can do to improve our instructional knowledge of research and practice.

One of my biggest insights has been that we educators need to observe what effective literacy practices look like in diverse schools and classrooms, hear the language of that responsive teaching, and discuss and analyze that teaching *before* we can apply those practices, in our own classrooms, with our own students. That knowledge was the driving force for developing my multiyear, video-based, literacy series for schools, principals, teachers, and literacy coaches (see www .regieroutman.com/inresidence/default.aspx/).

Take action

- **Seek to make professional conversations integral to school life**. Highly achieving schools are sustained through ongoing literate conversations—throughout the school day—with highly informed teachers, coaches, specialists, principals, and other leaders. It is those probing, thoughtful, reflective conversations that drive "need to know" and that propel us forward.

- **Take responsibility for our own professional development**. Become a member of a professional organization such as the International Reading Association (IRA), National Council of Teachers of English (NCTE), or Association for Supervision and Curriculum Development (ASCD). As a school team that includes the principal, attend a local, state, or national conference together.

- **Collaborate with our colleagues**. When possible, plan with grade-level or content area colleagues. Collaborative conversations about what we see and hear professionally push and solidify our thinking (see "Read professionally," p. 16).

- **Participate in coaching experiences**. When we have developed a trusting school culture, coaching experiences with colleagues have the potential to improve teaching.

- **Reflect continuously upon our beliefs, practices, instruction, and learning**. Becoming an expert teacher is a continuing journey.

Create access to complex texts

I have been teaching reading for more than four decades—as an elementary classroom teacher, certified and experienced reading specialist, Reading Recovery teacher, teacher of students with learning disabilities, and mentor teacher. One thing I know for certain: Matching students with texts they can read and understand is crucial. Marie Clay's groundbreaking research taught us many years ago that steady diets of too-hard books make readers regress, not progress. So while the newest standards emphasize that all students read complex texts—a worthy and important goal—I'm concerned we may be expecting students to tackle complex texts before they are ready. As well, the recommendation that students do multiple readings of a complex text and figure things out for themselves with little guidance is off the mark if the text is at a student's frustration level. The best preparation for reading increasingly complex texts is wide background knowledge gained through successful experiences listening to, choosing, reading, investigating, questioning, discussing, and understanding a wide range of fiction and nonfiction texts, genres, and authors. We teachers provide some of those experiences for students (see the first bulleted item in this lesson's Take Action) but, mostly, as students become increasingly adept as readers, we continue to guide and support them to read and comprehend more intricate texts.

We educators must first be discerning readers of complex texts ourselves and be able to think aloud and explain how we problem solve and grasp difficult concepts before we can effectively teach our students to do the same. For that to happen, we must advocate for and receive professional development that explicitly shows us how to read, question, analyze, and deeply understand weighty texts. That expert modeling must follow the same Optimal Learning Model we use with students and include shared experiences, guidance, and lots of practice. One recommended way to begin is with a schoolwide "book study." Rich and lively discussions with colleagues have the potential to raise deep questions, intelligently consider weighty issues and ideas, encourage self-reflection, and develop teacher confidence for leading similar, high-level discussions with our students (see "Read and write more texts," p. 82).

Take action

- **Provide access for *all* to increasingly complex texts**—through daily reading aloud, thinking aloud, problem solving, providing needed background knowledge and explanation of crucial vocabulary and concepts and, especially, demonstrating and fostering the habits, behaviors, and strategies of competent readers to the whole class, small group, and individual.

◆ **Ensure students get daily, sustained reading practice on content-rich, relevant, age-appropriate books** that have just enough challenge so students can successfully figure out words, vocabulary, concepts, and text meanings. Without sustained practice on meaningful texts that students can read with at least 95% accuracy and 90% comprehension, comprehension will remain superficial.

◆ **Emphasize reading for meaning right from the start**. Reading the world begins at birth. Reading to learn begins the moment a child interacts with a text. Use shared reading experiences, guided reading, and, especially, one-on-one reading conferences to ensure students understand what they read and are not just pronouncing words.

Make parents our partners

Based on former school experiences, it can be very intimidating for parents and families just to walk into a school building. Consider welcoming signs, easy-to-read brochures of services the school offers, and, if possible, even a small room or space where parents can come to meet other parents, learn about school offerings and special programs, find out about opportunities for volunteers, sign out books on learning, learn how to best help with homework, and so on. Consider, also, working with the principal to offer an occasional "early morning coffee" for families, as a time to meet with the principal, available teachers, and other families to hear the news of the school. Socializing with the people we work with and depend on go a long way toward building trust within the school community. It's well known, in fact, that despite the media hype on the failure of our public schools, most parents give their local schools high grades. Parents and families are our strongest advocates, and we need to continually let them know we value them and are here to serve them.

Take action

- **Communicate clearly with families**. Use newsletters, e-mails, phone calls, and social media to let families know what we are teaching and what students are learning, what our explicit expectations are for students and their families, and the best way and times to reach us.

- **Welcome parents into the school**. Consider an "open learning time" for families every few months, when they are welcome to come into our classrooms for a specified time frame to observe and even participate in what's going on. Plan and carry out this time with students, and use it as an opportunity to showcase learning in the classroom, with students explaining to parents what they will see and what to especially notice. For example, if a shared writing lesson is planned, families could be asked to notice how all students' thinking is honored and how we collaborate with students to shape their thinking.

- **Let families know we value their students**. Initiate contact with parents and guardians early in the school year and occasionally throughout the school year. Use a phone call, text, e-mail, or personal communication to let them know something positive about their child. Then, if we need to make contact with a concern, they will be more likely to listen—without getting defensive—and to problem solve with us. As a wise colleague noted, "They don't care how much we know until they know how much we care."

Assess as we teach

Optimally, assessment, which is a systematic process of monitoring learning so we can determine what's going well and what needs improvement, is seamlessly interwoven into our daily teaching without overwhelming it. The most useful assessments are formative, which means they are classroom based, ongoing, and have the potential, if done well, to reliably inform and enhance our daily instruction as well as student learning, engagement, and motivation. Think about formative assessment as being continuous—that is, it occurs before, during, and after teaching. While summative assessment, which includes mostly district and states tests, is important for accountability purposes for the wider community, it is not very useful for analyzing or improving an individual student's growth or for making instructional decisions. More important, summative tests are often high stakes with accompanying sanctions and negative consequences, which often lead to overzealousness on test preparation. Michael Pollan (2009) wrote, in his often-quoted opening lines from *In Defense of Food*, "Eat food. Not too much. Mostly plants." Balance in assessment, as in eating, is key. I have rewritten Pollan's lines for us educators: "Assess kids. Not too much. Mostly teach."

Take action

- **Integrate assessment with teaching**. Think of assessment as an integral part of all effective instruction, including what we ask students to do when they are working independently. We must know and cannot assume that students are learning more without an assessment.

- **Do more formative assessment**. The most useful assessment is the meaningful probing, nudging, and thoughtful questions we ask—in the act of teaching—to let us know what students are thinking and learning and where we need to adjust our instruction. Such assessment is part of responsive teaching, where we listen and observe carefully and change course on our lessons—or not—based on learners' responses (See *Regie Routman in Residence* for exactly what that assessment-as-part-of-teaching looks and sounds like: www.regieroutman.com/inresidence/default.aspx. See also "Depend on formative assessment," p. 145).

- **Do more one-on-one conferring**. The word *assessment* comes from the Latin word *assidere*, which means "to sit by." Especially for improving achievement in reading and writing, meeting one-on-one with students is crucial. Some of these conferences are roaming conferences, done quickly on-the-run during literacy blocks; most take place with the teacher sitting right beside a student and, in other cases, a small group (see "Embrace public writing conferences," p. 78 and "Rely on one-on-one reading conferences," p. 158).

- **Provide feedback to the learner**. Assessment, to be effective, must help the learner, whether it's a teacher or student, learn more. Effective feedback is not praise or criticism. It is carefully chosen language and actions that propel the learner forward (see "Provide feedback that supports the learner," p. 80 and "Ask more vital questions," p. 12).

- **Teach self-assessment**. Even our youngest learners can be taught to self-check and take more responsibility for monitoring their reading and writing. Ask, "Is it right?" "How do you know?" "Where can you find out?" "Where does it tell you that?" Also, students can be taught and guided to write "I can" literacy statements that match a school's beliefs and practices and then to back up these statements with proof from their work.

Promote oral language development

Begin literacy instruction with rich and meaningful oral language—the literary and informational language of books and texts we read aloud and discuss, the stories we tell, the texts we create together, and the rich vocabulary and curriculum in which we immerse students. Students who grow up in poverty—many of whom are also English-language learners—often enter our schools with limited, academic oral language, which makes learning to read and write more difficult. While we cannot make up for the fewer words and conversations they may have experienced, as compared with middle class and affluent families, we must ensure their school experiences immerse them in a flood of rich, relevant, and explicit language experiences throughout the day—significant conversations, opportunities to try out new words, reading and writing text after text, small-group work, and whatever it takes early on and throughout their school experiences. A highly skilled English language development teacher put it this way: "My sole purpose is to make sure our students, all of them, become master language manipulators in order to communicate in whatever format they are using" (see "Support English-language learners," p. 64).

Take action

- **Communicate clearly with families**. Check to ensure families feel comfortable with our means of communication, the content, and the delivery. Translated materials and conversations, when necessary and possible, go a long way to effectively communicating and promoting inclusivity.

- **Reevaluate the school's English-language learning program.** Advocate to push-in and coteach rather than pull-out, when possible, so students maximize language-learning experiences. Teach whole-part-whole (see p. 101) with explicit skills and language objectives embedded into the content, which accelerates language learning and makes the language and content more accessible, relevant, and enjoyable for all students.

- **Invite students to tell the stories of their lives**—with our scaffolding and encouragement—through talk, illustrations, photos, dictation, writing, video, dramatization, music with lyrics (such as raps) and then, to publish, read, and perform many of these texts. Valuing students' stories and culture helps to diminish the boundaries between home and school, which makes it more likely that students will engage and flourish as literacy and language learners.

- **Use a child's oral language to create readable texts**, and make some of these bilingual. Often, a student's first reading may be his own written text. Our residency work shows that young students who write daily for authentic audiences and purposes readily learn phonemic awareness, all letters and sounds, spelling of high-frequency words, and a growing facility with language which extends to both reading and writing.

- **Promote avid reading**. The only way to "catch up" and learn the myriad concepts and vocabulary students must know to be "college and career ready" is to read widely in a variety of genres on a wide range of topics.

- **Do more partner work, turn-and-talk, and small group work**. Make sure many of these structures are heterogeneous so that emerging and struggling language learners have excellent language models to learn from. Frequent speaking opportunities are especially important for developing oral language capacities (see "Promote more opportunities for speaking," p. 160).

Advocate for saner practices

We must let our voices be heard. If our schools and districts are pressuring us to act in ways that disadvantage or harm a student or group of students or us educators, we have a moral responsibility to speak up, make suggestions, and lobby for alternative, beneficial approaches. It takes courage, fortitude, and data to resist policies that are not good for our students or us, but we have the responsibility to, at least, attempt to create more favorable and sensible options. We need to ask tough questions before new district adoptions, put students' needs before schedules, demonstrate and share more sensible approaches, and circumvent rules that constrain, when we can.

Take action

- **Adopt a "can do" spirit**. I will never forget planning our first Urgency and School Change Conference in collaboration with Seattle University in Washington. We ran into continual roadblocks because of the university's strict procedures and policies. Yet each time we seemed to hit an insurmountable barrier, the associate dean stayed positive and took the attitude, "We'll find a way to work around this obstacle," and she did, every time. "All things can be made possible." That upbeat spirit pervaded the conference and needs to pervade our daily teaching.

- **Resist learned helplessness**. Even when schools and educators find out a practice has little or no benefits for students, the practice often continues because we don't know what else to do. One example has been the continuing use of DIBELS, despite reams of data that show questionable benefits (see *Teaching Essentials* website: www.regieroutman.com/teachingessentials/DIBELS.asp). In another example, a competent teacher I knew well shared with me that her new, inexperienced, and well-intentioned principal had "devastated" her with a poor evaluation and, in particular, with the scathing language that had been put in writing. Rather than continue to feel helpless and defeated, I suggested she model for her principal the language and actions that would be helpful in moving her teaching forward. The teacher was able to shift her stance from "I can't work with this principal" to "I'm going to

142

advocate for what I need." Her next observation and written evaluation were highly positive.

◆ **Advocate for our students**. Sometimes it comes down to this: We are the only ones who can effectively advocate for more responsible and effective practices, resources, and instructional and assessment approaches. Do whatever we can to ensure all our students are having their needs met in a successful, respectful, and equitable manner.

Be efficient

I'm a clock watcher when I teach. Demonstration: I make sure I don't go on longer than 10–15 minutes. Directions: I self-monitor my language to ensure it is concise, clear, and relevant to the task. Pacing: I try to stop an activity while interest is still high, which makes it easier to return to it the following day if we need to. Highly effective educators are highly efficient. We avoid busywork, worksheets and assignments that aren't worth the time they take, complicated directions, and long transitions between activities, to name a few tricks of the trade. Being efficient and not wasting a minute allows for more guided and sustained practice time, which is essential for mastering anything worthwhile, as well as for more instructional time. Perhaps, most important, we can't be efficient if we're not really good at what we're doing, which includes not just literacy and content knowledge but also management and organization.

Take action

- Don't go on too long
- Give clear, concise directions
- Aim for excellent pacing
- Avoid distractions that take us off task
- Plan relevant lessons
- Assess before teaching
- Use peer tutors and cross-grade tutors
- Be flexible; shift gears as needed
- Release more responsibility to students
- Have more student-directed groups
- Do an excellent job frontloading
- Plan with the end in mind
- Stick with what's most important at this time
- Keep our eyes on the goal(s)

All of these tips are embedded in other lessons throughout this text, as being efficient is essential for being fully effective as an instructional teacher, leader, and coach.

Depend on formative assessment

If we are to be highly skillful as teachers, we must astutely observe, question, and respond to students' needs and interests as we instruct, minute-by-minute and day-by-day, in order to *inform* our instruction and adjust it, as needed. With such formative assessment, we constantly evaluate what students know and need to know so we can take the appropriate actions to guide and propel them to further competency and independence. Teachers who seamlessly integrate formative assessments into the daily life of the classroom are able to use ongoing assessments to modify, fine tune, differentiate, and accelerate instruction for all learners—often on the spot. Formative assessments can include but are not limited to probing questions, anecdotal records, running records, conferences (one-on-one, public, roving), responses to reading (see p. 30), on-demand writing, and oral and written self-assessments by individual students and small groups, and more.

Take action

- **Cultivate and act upon a formative assessment mind-set**. Such a mind-set depends on being professionally knowledgeable and perceptive so we can do the in-the-moment, inner self-questioning before, during, and after instruction to guide our next moves. Be thinking:

  - "What are the purposes and goals for this lesson?"
  - "What do students already know about...?"
  - "What demonstrations and shared experiences will they need to understand and apply...?"
  - "Are we building in enough frontloading and guided practice time?"
  - "What's our evidence that students are learning what we are teaching?"
  - "What are our next steps?"

- **Note trends and needs** and reteach, provide more shared experiences, regroup, or instruct and further assess, as necessary, to meet the needs of all students. One way to notice student engagement in reading is to have a student lead the class in a familiar shared reading, leaving us free to observe the participation and behaviors of every student.

- **Employ more self-assessments**, after first demonstrating and explaining our expectations, such as:

  - Oral or written self-evaluations by small groups or individual students
  - Portfolios—collections of student work over time to show evidence of learning, chosen by the student, at first, with teacher modeling and guidance
  - "I can" statements, backed up with evidence from students' work
  - Conferences where students restate their strengths and needs or write learning goals after they have been jointly set
  - Questions generated by students to demonstrate deep understanding of a topic
  - Practice tests where students self-score against a student-friendly rubric
  - Self-checks and self-corrections for accuracy in word work in reading and writing

Build stamina

My stamina for writing increases the more I write. That is, the more writing becomes a daily habit, the longer I can stay with the task and the more efficient and energetic I become as a writer. Building endurance depends on sufficient practice time, with something like an 80:20% ratio of practice to lesson. The amount of time actually practicing and doing the activity—whether it be writing, reading, researching, playing a sport, playing an instrument—must be the sustained activity itself, not the lesson or demonstration. Stamina requires that the underlying basics have been learned, for example, adequate handwriting for sustained writing, sufficient reading habits and strategies for independent reading, or the rudiments of playing an instrument. Stamina calls for sufficient know-how, determination, staying power, and resilience—all characteristics of successful people.

Take action

- **Let students know why stamina matters**. Say something like, "Today I'm going to expect you to work in your groups (or read independently, continue writing, take notes, sit on the carpet) for 30 minutes. We've slowly been building up stamina. Stamina is being able to stick with something and give it your full effort. Stamina is very important for becoming an excellent student, successful worker at a job, or for becoming a highly skilled athlete, musician, mathematician, dancer, scientist, and so on."

- **Start small**. Build up stamina slowly, day by day. For example, while young students may, at first, only be able to read or write on their own—or stay focused in group time—for 5–10 minutes, incremental increases over time can add up to 45–60 minutes day.

- **Connect stamina to effort**. Increased stamina is easier to attain when the activity or task is purposeful to us and we can visualize the end results. When we value the lesson or activity, we are more likely to persist at it, even in the face of difficulty. It's hard to develop stamina at something we don't want to do. This is as true for us educators as it is for students.

- **Give feedback**. Let students know when we notice their stamina increasing. Say something like, "I noticed you were able to work on your own and figure out your own solutions for a full hour today. When you take the state reading test, you will need that kind of stamina, and now you have it."

See our classrooms through students' eyes

What would it be like to spend a whole day in our classroom if we were the students? It's easy to organize our classrooms to fit our own needs and personal styles and to forget what it was like to be a child, preteen, adolescent, or even an adult learner. If we truly want students to excel, we need to be sure the setting, tone, and classroom culture encourage and enhance risk taking, deep conversations, and meaningful learning. We educators set the temperature and controls for learning. The language we use, the choices we make possible, the learning structures and supports we set up, and the way we foster peer relationships and collaboration are vital to learners' emotional and mental well-being, regardless of the age of the learner.

Take action

♦ **Evaluate access**. Ensure that selected resources—such as charts, word walls, dictionaries, libraries, websites—are top notch, student friendly, well organized, at eye level, readable, and easy to use and understand without too much teacher direction and guidance.

♦ **Look at opportunities for interaction**. It's difficult to sit quietly in one place for most of the day. Check that we are providing adequate time and space for movement, conversing with peers, working with a partner, being part of a small group for problem solving and discussion, and for hearing all the voices.

♦ **Consider whose classroom it is**. Make sure we are not giving the message that we own the classroom and that our students are our tenants for the year. Although the final decision may be ours, do involve students in deciding how the classroom is organized—the library, jobs, rules, bulletin boards, desk arrangement, small-group collaboration, work areas—so they feel some ownership and comfort in a space they reside in for part or most of their day.

♦ **Demonstrate empathy**. Imagine how it would feel not to understand the language, vocabulary, and concepts or to be a student who is new, hungry, unstable, overtired, or homeless. Would we feel at ease in our own classrooms?

How well would we fare? What can we do to ensure we and our students create a welcoming and thriving learning environment for all?

◆ **Self-evaluate**. At various intervals, give students a questionnaire or open-ended evaluation that does not require their signatures. Ask for feedback and advice on how being in the classroom has worked for them. Include topics, such as choice, respect, fairness, problem solving, teacher effectiveness, group work, and whatever seems important. Have students state first what is working well. Let them know that, like them, we are always seeking to do better, and we will take their comments and suggestions seriously.

Know important literacy research

Highly effective teachers and leaders know literacy research and how and when to question it. We have a strong foundation of knowledge for interpreting research and applying what fits and makes sense for our own teaching/learning/assessing contexts. We use excellent research to inform our instruction without directing it—that is, we consider the research in light of what we know about literacy, subject matter, instructional approaches, and our individual students. See the following Take Action bullet points for key research that we can use to support exemplary literacy practices. For much more on relevant research, see www.regieroutman.com/inresidence/research.aspx.

Take action

- Schools that are more collegial and collaborative have higher literacy achievement (Fullan & Hargreaves, 1996).
- Highly effective teachers have their students read and write meaningful, continuous texts throughout the day, assign purposeful and challenging tasks, and support students with explicit demonstrations and grouping practices (Allington, 2002).
- Reliance on telling teaching is not beneficial to students' reading comprehension. (Taylor et al., 2002). Responsive teaching, with guided questioning and ongoing formative assessment, leads to deeper, longer lasting achievement.
- Core reading programs are limited in their scope for effectively teaching reading comprehension (Dewitz et al., 2009). We teachers must take the lead in teaching reading for understanding.
- Expertly educated and trained kindergarten teachers can greatly increase the reading abilities of at-risk kindergartners (Allington, 2011).
- Teaching reading and writing as reciprocal processes improves and accelerates both reading and writing (Graham & Hebert, 2010).
- Learners read and write more complex texts when the reading and writing activities are authentic—that is, when the activity has a real-world purpose and audience (Duke et al., 2006).
- Writing enhances and deepens thinking and learning (Murray, 1996).

◆ Reading and writing more nonfiction texts lead to higher literacy achievement (Duke & Bennett-Armistead, 2003).

◆ The less knowledge teachers have about writing, the more that test prep becomes the writing focus (Hillocks, 2002).

◆ Excellent formative assessments (see p. 145) must be integrated into our daily teaching for optimal instruction and learning (Valencia, 2011).

Emphasize nonfiction—along with fiction

To function well in our complicated world, we need to read and understand more nonfiction and complex texts. The newest standards, the Common Core State Standards for college and career readiness, recognize that fact and emphasize nonfiction reading and writing. In fact, for most of us adults, nonfiction reading comprises at least 70% of the reading we do. I begin each day reading the newspaper for at least an hour. I read national and international news stories, editorials, letters to the editor, commentaries, and business articles along with reviews of books, technology, apps, movies, restaurants. During the day, I use the Internet to research, sift through information, clarify questions, learn about new websites, read educational blogs. As well, I read cooking magazines, educational and research journals, weekly and monthly magazines to which I subscribe, directions, procedures, and more. And, always I am reading excellent fiction and nonfiction books.

Recognizing the importance of nonfiction, I often begin our literacy work in a residency with informational texts, those we read to students, those we write together, and those they research and write through our demonstrations, shared experiences, and guided practice. Especially in schools where most of the students qualify for free and reduced-cost lunch, we use riveting nonfiction, often picture books, to increase oral language, background knowledge, content, and reading comprehension (see "Know important literacy research," p. 150).

Yet I am an avid and devoted fiction reader and worry that fiction may be deemphasized in our zeal for more informational reading and writing. It is, in fact, the close reading of fiction and understanding of complex characters and life situations that have helped me become a discerning nonfiction reader. History is about his story and her story, and the nonfiction that most resonates with me is a beautifully told story with one or more central characters that I get to know and understand. *Zeitoun* by Dave Eggers is one such gripping favorite. The reader comes to know and understand the full impact of Hurricane Katrina—the events, injustices, complexity, horror, and hope—through the eyes, actions, and thoughts of the main character, Abdulrahman Zeitoun, and his family.

My granddaughter Katie, a middle school student, has been a devoted and discerning fiction reader all her life. Although she is just now developing a taste for nonfiction, I do not worry about her readiness for college. What follows is an excerpt from an e-mail she wrote me:

> The reason I emailed you is because I just finished reading *Wonder* by R.J. Palacio, one of the books you gave me. I think it is really profound, and I've never ever read a book like it before.... It's very interesting, and it made me think very hard about the way we treat other people.... I think you should read the book, because I am dying to talk about it with someone! It's bursting with discussion topics. (personal communication, April 2012)

"Bursting with discussion topics." Katie's need to know more and "talk about it with someone" is what we want for all readers. Her close reading and deep understanding of fiction have prepared her well to read and grasp the complex texts she will increasingly encounter in nonfiction forms and formats.

Infuse the arts into teaching and learning

It's well known that the visual and performing arts have the potential to improve academic performance and student engagement, which is especially critical for students in our underperforming schools. Yet, sadly, art, music, and drama programs are routinely cut when budgets get slashed. For students who learn differently or who have had limited success with traditional school approaches, emphasizing the arts can positively and permanently affect their lives. I still fondly remember Paul, one of the most disabled and talented students with whom I'd ever worked. As a nonreader in fourth grade, we used his extraordinary artistic abilities as a way into his becoming a reader. Recording his deep knowledge about cars into a book—beginning with his remarkable and detailed drawings and then adding his own language through dictation to each illustrated page—his own art work served to jump-start his phonics learning and his reading abilities and, as well, to boost his standing among his peers. And, again, working in a school in California where almost all the students qualified for free and reduced-cost meals, most of whom were also English-language learners, students had just attended their first classical music concert, which was to be the district's last because of budget constraints. The students were so affected by the "new music" they heard that we successfully lobbied the school board, through letters and personal communications, to continue this annual program for future classes. The students learned not only the power of persuasive and argumentative writing, but also that they could have agency in their own lives.

Take action

- **Integrate the visual and performing arts into all we do**. Explicitly teach and expose our students to the work of artists, musicians, painters, performers, actors, dancers, and filmmakers and connect the influence of the arts to content area studies and fully lived lives.

- **Invite local artists, musicians, and performing artists into our schools**. Many artists are eager to give back to their communities and will do so without charge or for a minimal fee. Have students write persuasive letters of invitation for classroom visits, an evening program for families, day-long visits, or residency programs.

- **Include excellent texts about artists, musicians, dancers, and performers** in literature discussions, read-alouds, guided reading groups, content areas, and classroom libraries. Some outstanding favorites that celebrate the power of the arts are *My Name Is Georgia: A Portrait* by Jeanette Winter (a picture book on painter Georgia O'Keefe, for primary grades); *Sandy's Circus: A Story About Alexander Calder* by Tanya Lee Stone (a picture book for grades 1–4 on Calder's wire sculptures); *The Art of Miss Chew* by Patricia Polacco (a memoir and picture book for elementary grades); *To Dance: A Ballerina's Graphic Novel* by Siena Cherson Siegel (a graphic novel for upper elementary through high school); and *This Land Was Made for You and Me: The Life and Songs of Woody Guthrie* by Elizabeth Partridge (biography for grade 6 and up).

- **Encourage unique descriptive arts** for storytelling, displaying content knowledge, and completing major projects, which may include offering wide options incorporating the visual, musical, and performance arts, such as original use of media, graphics, illustrations, photos, paintings, videos, audio tools, songs, dances, film, and more—which make it more likely all students can successfully participate and present information in a way that respects their talents, learning styles, and cultural diversity.

Do more student-directed, small-group work

The longer I teach, the more I employ small-group work. Having small groups of students working together is ideal for extending shared experiences, giving every student an opportunity to speak, discuss, and fully participate, and building confidence before students attempt a task on their own. In my experience, heterogeneous groups of 3 or 4 students that are also balanced by gender work best. Groups can be revising a class-authored shared writing, composing an introduction to a research report, holding a literature conversation, problem solving in math, making scientific observations, and so on. Once we have laid sufficient groundwork with students, it's easy and time efficient to have multiple groups meeting at the same time—even in the primary grades. That frees us up to join one or more groups who need more explanation and guidance or to float among groups and take brief observational notes on strengths and needs. In self-directed, small-group work, students are in charge to responsibly collaborate and try out or refine what we have been teaching, so our expectations and guidelines need to be very clear. As well, we need to have done enough frontloading so students are successful with minimum guidance from us (For viewing detailed information on self-directed groups, see *Transforming Our Teaching Through Reading/Writing Connections*, session 7).

Take action

- **Establish guidelines**. Include procedures for expected behaviors, such as making eye contact, speaking politely and coherently, citing evidence to back up statements, respectfully adding on, agreeing with, or disagreeing with a speaker, and so on.
- **Demonstrate how groups work together**. Guide one student group while all other students look on. Use a fish-bowl demonstration, where we take on the role of group facilitator and lead the group to stay on task and ensure that every group member gets a chance to speak. Have onlookers jot down what they notice the facilitator and students doing well, which keeps students focused and also serves as our evaluation of the positive moves students take away from the observation. Also use the notes to create a rubric of student expectations.

- ◆ **Coach students on how to use the OLM**. Make the Optimal Learning Model (p. 15) explicit to students and encourage them to apply the model when working with peers and younger students.

- ◆ **Teach students to ask and answer their own vital questions**. Demonstrate the difference between open-ended questions, which encourage multiple responses as long as they are supported by evidence from the text, and closed questions, which usually have one right answer that is easily found in the text (see "Ask more vital questions," p. 12).

- ◆ **Have students self-evaluate** their behaviors for working productively together. Follow the OLM to gradually release responsibility to students as a group and, later, individually—to orally and, eventually, in writing—note their strengths, areas for improvements, and goals for next steps. As well, use students' self-evaluations to determine our own next steps.

Rely on one-on-one reading conferences

Make reading conferences a priority! Build in time for daily, monitored, independent reading! It is during this sustained practice time that students cement the strategies and techniques we've been demonstrating and guiding them to try out and apply to their daily reading. The best way to know if students are deeply comprehending is to sit side by side with them, observe them reading silently, and probe the depth of their understanding with thoughtful questions. Then we can truly ascertain what students know and need to know and plan our and their next steps and goals. We are turning out lots of superficial readers who move through levels but who never become proficient. Although reading levels and computerized tests can provide data, we can easily be lulled into a false sense of complacency with numbers that move upwards while students continue to spend time with books they minimally understand. Too often our students are able to read the words and retell a story with lots of details but are unable to infer, summarize, analyze, or distill the text's most important ideas.

Use daily sustained reading time to confer one-on-one with students. For optimal comprehension, have the student bring a book-in-process or recently completed text to the reading conference. Because almost all the reading we do in the world is silent, except for beginning readers, have the student read a page or two silently while we do the same and observe students' actions. Plan to record in detail the content and results of the conference and use the record keeping to share with students and their families and keep as part of our ongoing, formative assessment. (For detailed information on reading conferences, see *Reading Essentials*, pp. 100–111 and view videos in *Transforming Our Teaching Through Reading to Understand* for procedures, questions to ask, and teaching points to make. See, also, "Tell the truth," p. 115).

Take action

Important factors to assess for deep understanding include, but are not limited to, the following:

- Choosing and accessing appropriate and readable text—reading level, content, layout, organization, genre, strategies used in selection of text, knowledge of author and genre, going beyond the "five-finger test"
- Reading with fluency and a suitable rate, connected to type of text

- Figuring out unknown words—applying word-study skills
- Summarizing
- Inferring meaning that is backed up by text evidence and experiences
- Handling of unknown vocabulary
- Having a plan of action when meaning breaks down, such as rereading or seeking and using appropriate strategies and resources
- Understanding of character development, motivation, and change—in fiction and in biography and history texts
- Determining, retrieving, and consolidating important information and facts
- Self-evaluating reading strengths and needs and setting important goals

Promote more opportunities for speaking

I'll never forget how terrified I was when I began publicly speaking to educators decades ago. Looking back, a big part of my fright was my total lack of experience. In all my years of schooling I was reticent to speak out in classes and recall little encouragement or guidance to do so. Not surprisingly, my lack of experience greatly affected my initial confidence and competence. When I had the good fortune to hear and observe esteemed writing educator Donald Graves speak to a large audience, I thought I had found my speaking answer. He spoke animatedly and confidently without notes, and his seamless presentation appeared effortless. Naïvely, I believed that Don's casual and personal presentation style was one I could emulate without too much added work to my full-time teaching schedule. How wrong I was! Little did I know until he invited me to copresent with him that he spent countless months and hours on meticulous planning and practice to pull off that "effortless" presentation. Just like anything complex that we learn to do extremely well, it takes hundreds if not thousands of hours of practice over many years to become expert. To be an effective and engaging speaker, one must be knowledgeable and pay close attention to the appropriateness and relevance of the content, the needs and interests of the audience, the pacing of the talk, what's most important to say and how to say it in a limited time frame, possible technology support, and much more. Unfortunately, it is still rare to walk into a classroom and see and hear rich issue-related discussion that is primarily directed by students. Yet such ongoing dialogue is a needed shift for us. Being a competent, clear communicator and being able make an effective and persuasive argument are necessities for interacting successfully with others and for giving useful feedback in life and in work.

Take action

- **Demonstrate, analyze, and apply what effective speakers do**. Listen to and view excellent media forms such as highly effective video and audio talks, for example, TED talks for students, which are limited to fewer than 20 minutes and are mostly done without notes (See TED talks websites: www.ted .com/talks, ed.ted.com/). With our guidance, chart together what we observe. Discuss what students and we might be able to try and apply.

- ◆ **Notice what successful speakers often do**:
  - Demonstrate knowledge of the topic and stay on topic
  - Display enthusiasm and energy in talking about the topic, question, or issue
  - Make the purpose of their talk clear and relevant
  - Customize their talk for a specific audience
  - Make points succinctly and clearly and back them up with evidence
  - Know what's most important to include and to leave out
  - Have a closure that listeners can remember
- ◆ **Promote significant conversations across the curriculum**
  - Have students, with preestablished classroom guidelines, explain their thinking on a project they've completed, problem they've solved, or topic they've learned about. Have students practice their presentations in small groups prior to speaking to the whole class. Demonstrate how to give authentic and useful feedback.
  - Set up weekly book talks where students can sign up to give a book talk to convince others to read a favorite text. Establish criteria and time limits ahead of time. Demonstrate first, with a read-aloud all students are familiar with, what an excellent book talk sounds like.
  - Give more time for small-group work, which affords more speaking opportunities (see p. 156).
  - Make literature conversations part of the reading curriculum.

Teach students, not standards

I f we are not professionally proactive and knowledgeable, preparing students for the latest standards will become our teaching focus rather than meeting the educational needs and interests of all of our students. Already, in response to the call for reading and responding to more complex texts, numerous states are spending countless hours poring over their basal texts to figure out deeper meanings and to create "text-dependent" questions for their core reading selections. Spending more time with basal texts is surely not the best route to go! Also, keep in mind that there is no research that shows that states that have adopted high standards fare any better than those with low standards (Loveless, 2012). We educators are the ones who need to be on the front lines in determining the high-quality curriculum that respects our students' cultural and language identities and that provides the significant and targeted scaffolding learners require. We simply cannot assume that adopting standards will cause students to learn more. We must make certain that it is our highly informed interpretation of standards—and not publishers' materials that proclaim to align with standards—that lead the way.

Yet although the newest standards specify that what can or should be taught is determined by teachers and curriculum developers, this is both good news and bad news. The good news is that we educators have the freedom to decide "the how" of teaching. The not-so-good-news is that too few of us have sufficient professional expertise and necessary time to choose and develop curriculum, resources, and approaches to help guide students reach the higher literacy, literature, and informational benchmarks. For many of us, our lack of knowledge makes us vulnerable to overrelying on standards and outside forces instead of ourselves. What we need in every school and district are embedded learning communities that push our professional thinking and practices in ways that make us highly competent teachers, assessors, and decision makers who truly believe in what we are doing. We teachers and administrators need to establish and sustain learning environments that are collaborative, meaningful, authentic, and compelling in teaching, assessing, and applying excellent literacy practices across the curriculum. Here, it is crucial that principals are a part of the learning communities and lead by example. Not to be minimized, all of the aforementioned require a steadfast commitment to fund, support, and trust the professional learning process and to give it time to become an integral part of the culture of the school or district.

A call to action

We must do everything we can to stay focused on the students in front of us and to give them the excellent education that is their birthright. They, not standards, are why we're here. Take the lead to ensure that our colleagues and we invest in school-wide professional learning that makes us smart, savvy, and wise. It is our obligation as responsible educators to continue to grow and become more effective at our craft. If we are not continuously learning, questioning, reflecting, and rethinking, we are likely to accept the status quo or settle for complacency. As highly informed and knowledgeable educators, let us vow to stay on the front lines for literacy and learning excellence, vigilance, and sound professional judgment. Our students are counting on us, and we can't let them down. We can do it!

References

Allington, R. (2002). What I've learned about effective reading instruction from a decade of studying exemplary elementary classroom teachers. *Phi Delta Kappan, 83*(10), 740–747.

Allington, R. (2011). What at-risk readers need. *Educational Leadership, 68*(6), 40–45.

Cooper, H.M. (2006). *The battle over homework: Common ground for administrators, teachers, and parents.* Thousand Oaks, CA: Corwin.

Darling-Hammond, L., & Richardson, N. (2009). Teacher learning: What matters? *Educational Leadership, 66*(5), 46–55.

Dewitz, P., Jones, J., & Leahy, S. (2009). Comprehension strategy instruction in core reading programs. *Reading Research Quarterly, 44*(2), 102–126.

Duke, N., & Bennett-Armistead, S. (2003). *Reading and writing informational texts in the primary grades: Research-based practices.* New York: Scholastic.

Duke, N.K., Caughlan, S., Juzwik, M., Martin, N. (2012). *Reading and writing genre with purpose in K–8 classrooms.* Portsmouth, NH: Heinemann.

Duke, N., Purcell-Gates, V., Hall, L.A., & Towers, C. (2006). Authentic literacy activities for developing comprehension and writing. *The Reading Teacher, 60*(4), 344–355.

Dweck, C.S. (2007). *Mindset: The new psychology of success.* New York: Random House.

Fullan, M., & Hargreaves, A. (1996). *What's worth fighting for in your school?* (Rev. ed.). New York: Teachers College Press.

Gawande, A. (2007). Better: A surgeon's notes on performance. New York: Metropolitan.

Gawande, A. (2011, October 3). Personal best: Annals of medicine. *The New Yorker*, pp. 44–53.

Graham, S., & Hebert, M. (2010). *Writing to read: Evidence for how writing can improve reading.* New York: Carnegie Corporation.

Guskey, T.B., & Suk Yoon, K. (2009). What works in professional development? *Phi Delta Kappan, 90*(7), 495–507.

Hammond, W.D., & Nessel, D.D. (2011). *The comprehension experience: Engaging readers through effective inquiry and discussion.* Portsmouth, NH: Heinemann.

Hillocks, G. (2002). *The testing trap: How state writing assessments control learning.* New York: Teachers College Press.

Loveless, T. (2012). *How well are American students learning? With sections on predicting the effect of the Common Core State Standards, achievement gaps on the two NAEP tests, and misinterpreting international test scores.* (The Brown Center on Educational Policy, Trans.; Vol. 3, pp. 1–36). Washington, DC: Brookings Institute.

Murray, D.M. (1996). *Crafting a life in essay, story, poem.* Portsmouth, NH: Heinemann.

National Governors Association Center for Best Practices & Council of Chief State School Officers. (2010). *Common Core State Standards for English language arts and literacy in history/social studies, science, and technical subjects.* Washington, DC: Authors.

Pearson, P.D., & Gallagher, M.C. (1983). The instruction of reading comprehension. *Contemporary educational psychology, 8*, 317–344.

Pink, D. (2011). *Drive: The surprising truth about what motivates us.* New York: Penguin.

Routman, R. (1988). *Transitions: From literature to literacy.* Portsmouth, NH: Heinemann.

Routman, R. (2000). *Conversations: Strategies for teaching, learning, and evaluating.* Portsmouth, NH: Heinemann.

Routman, R. (2003). *Reading essentials: The specifics you need to know to teach reading well.* Portsmouth, NH: Heinemann.

Routman, R. (2005). *Writing essentials: Raising expectations and results while simplifying teaching.* Portsmouth, NH: Heinemann.

Routman, R. (2008a). *Teaching essentials: Expecting the most and getting the best from every learner, K–8.* Portsmouth, NH: Heinemann.

Routman, R. (2008b). *Regie Routman in residence: Transforming our teaching through writing for audience and purpose.* Portsmouth, NH: Heinemann.

Routman, R. (2008c). *Regie Routman in residence: Transforming our teaching through reading/writing connections.* Portsmouth, NH: Heinemann.

Routman, R. (2009). *Regie Routman in residence: Transforming our teaching through reading to understand.* Portsmouth, NH: Heinemann.

Taylor, B., Peterson, D.S., Pearson, P.D., & Rodriguez, M. (2002). Looking inside classrooms: Reflecting on the "how" as well as the "what" in effective reading instruction. *The Reading Teacher, 56*(3), 270–279.

Valencia, S.W. (2011). Using assessment to improve teaching and learning. In S.J. Samuels & A.E. Farstrup (Eds.), *What Research Has to Say About Reading Instruction* (4th ed., pp. 379–405). Newark, DE: International Reading Association.

Literature Cited

Bauermeister, E. (2009). *The school of essential ingredients.* New York: Putnam.

DeGross, M. (1994). *Donovan's word jar.* New York: Harper Trophy.

Eggers, D. (2009). *Zeitoun.* New York: Vintage.

Frasier, D. (2000). *Miss Alaineus: A vocabulary disaster.* New York: Scholastic.

Holland, J.S. (2011). *Unlikely friendships: 47 remarkable stories from the animal kingdom.* New York: Workman.

Larson, K., & Nethery, M. (2008). *Two Bobbies. A true story of Hurricane Katrina, friendship, and survival.* New York: Walker.

Palacio, R.J. (2012). *Wonder.* New York: Knopf.

Partridge, E. (2002). *This land was made for you and me: The life and songs of Woody Guthrie.* New York: Viking.

Polacco, P. (2012). *The art of Miss Chew.* New York: Putnam.

Polan, M. (2009). *In defense of food: An eater's manifesto.* New York: Penguin.

Rayn, P.M. (2002). *When Marian sang: The true recital of Marian Anderson.* New York: Scholastic.

Shoveller, H. (2006). *Ryan and Jimmy: And the well in Africa that brought them together.* Toronto, ON, Canada: Kids Can.

Siegel, S.C. (2006). *To dance: A ballerina's graphic novel.* New York: Atheneum.

Stone, T.L. (2008). *Sandy's circus: A story about Alexander Calder.* New York: Viking.

Strout, E. (2008). *Olive Kitteridge.* New York: Random House.

Thimmesh, C. (2011). *Friends: True stories of extraordinary animal friendships.* New York: Houghton Mifflin Harcourt.

Winter, J. (1998). *My name is Georgia: A portrait.* Orlando, FL: Harcourt.

Index

A

access to books, 112–113

achievement: of colleagues, acknowledging, 6; gap in, 3, 133; relationships and, 5, 123; of students, and expectations, 3, 40, 127

acknowledging: colleagues, 6, 11, 28, 69; heroes, 75–76; students, 36, 69

adults in school community: celebrating acts of kindness by, 76; respecting, 43; socializing with, 69; viewing as learners, 46

advocacy: for appropriate use of standards, 162; for better practices and resources, 14, 57, 64, 65, 94, 117, 118, 124, 142–143

Allington, Richard, 54, 82, 150

arts, integrating, 154–155

assessment: of comprehension through reading conferences, 101–102; for deep understanding of text, 158–159; definition of, 138; formative, 125, 138, 145–146, 158–159; during guided reading, 30; integration of with teaching, 138–139; of learning, 30, 31, 50, 73; of self-management by students, 32; summative, 138; through asking questions, 12–13, 24; through rubrics. See also self-assessment; self-evaluation

assignments: designing appropriate homework, 91–92; providing choice within framework of, 23; short writing assignments, 70

assumptions: about background knowledge, 62–63; about intelligence of students, 117

authenticity of instruction, 7–8, 20, 54, 61, 71; research on, 150

author, website of. See website of author

author's craft, noticing and applying, 41, 61, 93

B

background knowledge: assumptions about, 62–63; building on, 64; complex texts and, 135

behaviors: inappropriate, dealing with, 17–18; modeling, explaining, and practicing expected behaviors, 32; off-task, dealing with, 77; reducing need for intervention for, 114; solving classroom-based issues, 94–95. See also management

beliefs, developing shared, 98, 131–132. See also instructional beliefs and practices

Bennett-Armistead, S., 151

Better (Gawande), 33

better job, seeking to do, 33. See also commitment to do better

blogs, 47, 71, 72, 103

bonding with students and colleagues, 21

book reviews, 44, 93

book talks, 161

books: about artists, musicians, dancers, and performers, 155; conversations about, 130; leveling, 113; picture books, recommended, 93; for reading aloud, 41; sharing favorite, 21; student-authored, 45, 82–83; for vocabulary development, 107; writing, 57. See also texts

bulletin boards, 9, 23; posted information in schools, 131–132

C

Cameron, James, 66

"can do it" book list, 93

"can do" spirit, adopting, 142

Caughlan, S., 7

CCSS (Common Core State Standards), 48–49, 152

celebration: of acts of kindness, 76; as part of daily life, 121; of strengths, 21, 38, 46; viewing as teaching, 111; in writing conferences, 79

change: expectations for, 100; focusing energy where results are most likely, 127–128; hope for, 90; as taking time, 69; through celebration, 111; whole school, 2

charts, 9 , 52, 131. *See also* bulletin boards; word walls; resources

choice, providing within structure, 23, 50

classrooms: celebration as part of daily life of, 121; environment of, 9–10; libraries in, 9, 112–113; routines and rituals in, 120–121; solving issues in, 94–95; viewing through students' eyes, 148–149; word-conscious, 108. *See also* culture of schools and classrooms

Clay, Marie, 135

coaching relationships, 33, 59, 97, 134

collaboration, 97; research on, 150. *See also* colleagues; professional development; small-group work

colleagues: acknowledging, 6, 28, 69; collaboration with, 5, 97, 134; conversations with, 58, 134, 135; getting to know, 11; relationships with, 21; sharing best ideas with, 28. *See also* coaching relationships

college and career readiness, 48, 153. *See also* standards

commitment to do better; 3, 33, 40. *See also* determination to learn; expectations of students, raising; persistence, rewarding; urgency, teaching with a sense of

Common Core State Standards (CCSS), 3, 48–49, 152. *See also* standards

common language, using, 132

common sense, using, 124, 127

communication: with families, 137, 140; using technology for, 71–72. *See also* conversations; families

complex texts: creating access to, 49, 136; emphasizing, 152–153, 162; research on, 150

compliments, giving before suggestions, 46. *See also* celebration; feedback

comprehension, reading, 124, 129–130, 136; checking through writing, 30. *See also* complex texts; formative assessment; guided reading; questioning; reading; reading conferences

conferring with students: as assessment, 139; celebration in, 111; one-on-one, 139; public writing conferences, 78–79; reading conferences, 113, 115–116, 158–159

conversations: about texts, 29; with peers, 16, 58, 134, 135; scaffolded, 104–105; significant, promoting, 129–130, 161; "turn and talk" time, 34, 50, 129

Conversations (Routman), 130, 156

Cooper, Harris, 91

core literacy programs: limitations of, 84, 117; overreliance on, 124; research on, 150

courage, 98, 124. *See also* advocacy for better practices and resources

critical thinking, 49

Csikszemtmihalyi, Mihaly, 106

culture of school and classroom, 5, 11, 37, 58–59, 64, 162; self-evaluating, 108; word conscious classroom, 108. *See also* classrooms

current events, discussing, 63

curriculum: choosing texts, 61; extensive writing across, 49; interests and needs of students in, 11, 40, 114, 132; management focus and, 31; significant conversations across, 161; word study across, 51–52. *See also* beliefs; core literacy programs; reading; resources; writing

D

Darling-Hammond, L., 133

deficit mentality, discarding, 46. *See also* expectations of students, raising demonstrations and modeling: frontloading, 73; importance of, 19–20; literate conversations, 129; public speaking, 160; rereading and, 27; research process, 66; small-group work, 156; for teachers, 135; writing, 70. *See also* Optimal Learning Model

determination to learn, instilling, 22

Dewitz, P., 124, 150

DIBELS, 142

directions, giving: for ELLs, 65; listening skills and, 34

discussions, 34, 35, 63. *See also* conversations; questioning

distractions, eliminating, 94–95

"Dreams" topic, 60

Drive (Pink), 24

Duke, N., 7, 150, 151

Dweck, Carol, 36

E

editing work, 86–87

editorials, writing, 57, 72

edutopia.org website, 72

efficiency, striving for, 144–145

effort, connecting stamina to, 147

ELLs. *See* English-language learners

empathy, demonstrating, 148–149

energy, focusing where results are likely, 127–128

engagement: assessment of, 145; hearts, capturing, before teaching, 11; strategies for, 50; with technology use, 72

English-language learners (ELLs): comprehensible input, 65; evaluating school's program, 140; promotion of oral language development, 140–141; scaffolded conversations for, 104; supporting, 64–65; texts for, 61; vocabulary development, 107–108

environment, creating useful and beautiful space, 9–10

essential ingredients for becoming expert literacy teachers, 84

esteem for every learner, 123

excellence: in first instruction for all students, 117–118; as goal, 24

exemplars, 23, 82

expectations of students: raising, 40, 54, 60, 86, 90, 100; stating clear and reasonable, 95, 119

expert teaching, focusing on, 88–89. *See also* teaching, knowledgeable teachers

F

families: bonding with, 21; communication with, 137, 140; homework and, 91–92; as partners, 137; promoting reading aloud by, 42; sharing progress with, 89; treating with respect, 43, 76; welcoming message to, 43, 71, 137

feedback: defined, 139; effective, and assessment, 139; on increased stamina, 147; that supports learners, 80–81; in writing conferences, 79. *See also* language, choosing; positive feedback

fiction, reading, 152–153

flow and seamless teaching, 106

fluency, reading, 29, 31, 82, 158

formative assessment, 125, 138, 145–146; defined, 138; examples of, 145; research on, 159. *See also* assessment; feedback; questioning; self-assessments

foundation, building strong, 14, 84, 150

framework, for learning, 14, 23

Friends (Thimmesh), 58

frontloading, importance of, 73–74, 98. *See also* demonstrations and modeling

Fullan, M., 150

G

Gallagher, M.C., 15

Gawande, Atul, 33

genres, 44, 49, 70, 93

gradual release of responsibility, 15. *See also* Optimal Learning Model

Graham, S., 150

Graves, Donald, 160

group thinking, valuing, 36

groups, working in, 35, 109. *See also* small-group work
guided reading: Optimal Learning Model and, 15; sustained independent reading practice and, 29–30
Guskey, T.B., 133

H
Hammond, W.D., 129
handwriting, 96
Hargreaves, A., 150
hearts, capturing, before teaching, 11, 17
Hebert, M., 150
heroes, acknowledging, 75–76
Hillocks, G., 151
Holdaway, Don, 21
homework, designing and assigning, 91–92
hope, maintaining, 90

I
ideas: accepting all, 109; sharing, 122
imagination, providing time, space, and resources for, 53
improvement, seeking, 33. *See also* commitment to do better
independence, encouraging, 119
independent reading, connecting reading conferences to, 113, 158–159. *See also* sustained independent reading practice
informational text: close and deep reading of, 49; reading, 152–153; real-world, use of, 7
inquiry. *See* investigation
inspiring stories, sharing, 93. *See also* stories, telling, importance of
instructional beliefs and practices: advocacy for, 117, 124, 142–143; aligning resources with, 127; foundation of, 14; overview of, 1–2; shared, developing, 64, 131–132
instructional time, reevaluating, 68
intelligence of students, assuming, 117
interaction, opportunities for, 148
intervention, reducing need for, 114, 117
invented spelling, 87

investigation: asking vital questions, 12–13; creating a need to know, 66–67

J–K
Jones, J., 124
joy of teaching, 68–69
Juzwik, M., 7
kindergarten: observing excellent teachers, 54–55, 58; playtime, 54; research on, 150; students self-checking high frequency words, 51–52
kindness, acts of: celebrating, 6, 76; performing, 6
"knowledge sifters," 16

L
labels, avoiding, 117, 118
language: body language, 39; oral language, promoting, 140–141; in rubrics, 99; suggesting to students, 104–105. *See also* scaffolded conversations
language, choosing: affirmative, 46; for bonding with students and colleagues, 21; for feedback, 56, 79, 80; for literacy terms, 132; reading aloud and, 41; telling truth, 115–116; for writing conferences, 38–39
leadership, of teachers and principals, 3, 5, 59, 122, 142, 162
leadership teams, 97, 122
Leahy, S., 124
learned helplessness, resisting, 142–143
learners. *See* self-determining learners; students
leveling books, 61, 113
libraries in classrooms: organizing and setting up, 9; setting up and maintaining, 112–113
life, living interesting, 69, 103
listening, active, 34–35
literacy, integrated model of, 44
literacy research, knowledge of, 14, 150–151
Loveless, T., 162

M

management practices: during guided reading, 30; integration of into instruction, 31–32, 77

Martin, N., 7

meaning: connecting instruction with, 64–65; reading for, 136. *See also* authenticity

mentors, searching out, 58

modeling. *See* demonstrations and modeling; frontloading; Optimal Learning Model

motivation. *See* engagement

Murray, Donald, 57, 150

N

National Governors Association Center for Best Practices & Council of Chief State School Officers, 44

"need to know," creating in students, 66–67

Nessel, D.D., 129

nonfiction materials: choosing, 93; in classroom library, 112; close and deep reading of, 49, 152–153; real-world, use of, 7, 152; research on, 150

notebooks: for assessment, 30; reflection, 56

notes, handwritten, 96

O

objectives: learning, 65; related to planning, 17–18

Olive Kitteridge (Strout), 47

Optimal Learning Model (OLM): coaching students on use of, 66, 157; defining and applying, 15; in residencies, 2; scaffolded conversations in, 104. *See also* language

oral language development, promoting, 140–141

P

parents. *See* families

partner reading, 26, 31

partnerships: with families, 137; forming for coaching, 59

Pearson, P.D., 15, 82

performance arts, integrating, 154–155

persistence, rewarding, 36–37

Peterson, D., 82

Pink, Daniel, 24

planning time, reevaluating, 68

planning with end in mind, 17–18

poetry, reading and writing, 44, 70

Pollan, Michael, 138

portfolios, 146

positive feedback: to families, 21, 137; sharing, 123; to student writers, 79; that supports learners, 80–81; viewing as teaching, 111. *See also* feedback practices. *See* instructional beliefs and practices; management practices

principals: knowledge of literacy of, 122; in learning communities, 162; working with, 59, 97, 142. *See also* leadership

problem-solving, by students; 94–95. *See also* investigation

process, focusing on, 88

professional development: collaboration with colleagues, 5, 97, 134; components of, 135; equitable literacy focus and, 114; as fragmented and superficial, 62; implementation of standards and, 48; inviting all staff to, 43; leadership on, 64, 122; membership in professional organizations, 134; mentors, searching out, 58; as priority, 114, 133–134, 163; *Regie Routman in Residence*, ix, 2, 8, 122, 131, 138, 156, 158; "teach less, learn more" motto, 85; through residencies, 2–3, 100. *See also* coaching relationships; collaboration

professional learning communities, 133, 162. *See also* professional development

professional reading, importance of, 16

programs: as framework, 84; overreliance on, 124, 127. *See also* core literacy programs

public speaking, providing opportunities for, 160–161

public writing conferences, 78–79

publishing: for authentic audiences and purposes, 8; class-authored and student-authored work, 82; with correct spelling and conventions, 86; handwritten pieces, 96; posted work, 10; short writing assignments, 70; using technology, 71–72

pull-out models vs. push-in, 64–65, 117, 118, 121

purpose of instruction, 7–8, 125. *See also* authenticity

Q–R

questioning: asking vital questions, 12–13; as assessment, 30, 62–63, 138; in creating need to know, 66–67; to develop self-determining learners, 24; ELLs, 65; encouraging, 62; inauthentic resources, 8; open-ended questions, 12; responses to comprehension questions, 30; teaching students to ask and answer own questions, 25, 157

Readers Theatre, 26

reading: authentic and continuous texts, 82–83; connecting with writing, 41, 44–45; guided, 15, 29–30; professional, 16; "right" texts for, 61; shared reading, 125–126; vocabulary development and, 107. *See also* sustained independent reading practice

reading comprehension. *See* comprehension, reading

reading aloud: choosing quality literature, 93; as practice, 41–42; shared, 125–126; student pieces in public writing conferences, 78–79

reading conferences: connecting to independent reading, 113, 115–116; one-on-one, 158–159. *See also* assessment; questioning

Reading Essentials (Routman), 9, 126, 158

Reading Recovery, 46

reading-writing connection: importance of, 41, 44–45, 61; research on, 150; viewing, 156

ReadWriteThink.org website, 72

reflection: taking time for, 56–57, 68; through self-questioning, 81

Regie Routman in Residence professional development projects, ix, 2, 8, 97, 131, 138, 156, 158

relationships of trust and caring, importance of, 5, 11, 21, 58–59, 69

rereading: encouraging, 126; importance of, 26–27; when reading aloud, 41

research in literacy, knowledge of, 14, 150–151

research process, demonstrating, 66

residency model, 2–3, 17, 60, 97, 100, 112, 127

resources: advocacy for, 117, 124, 142–143; aligning with instructional beliefs and practices, 25, 127; availability of, 119; choosing excellent texts, 61; created from shared writing, 110; evaluating access to, 148; for imagination, 53; judicious use of, 124; for kindergarten, 55; questioning inauthentic, 8; for students, 87

respect for others, 5, 6, 43, 123

responsive teaching, telling teaching compared to, 66

restaurant reviews, 51

revising drafts, 27, 66. *See also* writing

rewarding: persistence, 36–37; thinking, 24. *See also* celebration

Richardson, N., 133

Rodriguez, M., 82

routines and rituals, 119, 120–121

Routman, R., 1–2, 8, 9, 15, 70, 80, 97, 109, 126, 130, 156. *See also Regie Routman in Residence* professional development projects; website of author

rubrics, creating and using, 99, 110

S

scaffolded conversations, 104–105. *See also* conversations; language, choosing

schedules and student needs, 59, 118, 121

The School of Essential Ingredients (Bauermeister), 84

schools: achievement in, 22, 41, 82, 90, 101; high needs schools, 60, 100, 154

seamless teaching, aiming for, 106

self-assessment, 51, 119, 139; examples of, 146

self-checking: for increasing independence, 119; spelling, 52

self-determining learners: defined, 2; developing, 24–25

self-directed groups, 156–157

self-evaluation: of classrooms, 149; of questioning, 12; with rubrics, 99; in small groups, 157. *See also* assessment

self-management by students, assessment of, 32

self-questioning, 12–13

senses, involving, 65

shared beliefs, developing, 131–132. *See also* instructional beliefs and practices

shared experiences, 15, 73, 156. *See also* scaffolded conversations; shared reading; shared writing

shared reading, 125–126

shared writing, 109–110; as assessment, 91

sharing: best ideas, 28; inspiring stories, 93

Singapore Schools, 85

Singleton, Marty, 123

skills, teaching, 84; in isolation, 102; in core reading programs, 124. *See also* whole-part-whole teaching; word study

slowing down to "hurry up" learning, 98

small-group work: assessment of, 36; to assign further reading, 31; establishing guidelines for, 35; to increase independence, 119; student-directed, 109, 156–157

Smith, Frank, 28

social media sites: sharing ideas on, 28; uses for, 71–72

speaking, promoting opportunities for effective, 160–161. *See also* conversations; listening; shared experiences; shared writing

special needs: of all learners, recognizing, 60; overidentification of students with, 114

spelling: expectations for, 86–87; invented spelling, 87; self-checking, 51, 52

stamina, building, 147

standards: going beyond, 18; implementing, 48–49, 85; for nonfiction reading and writing, 152; overreliance on, 162; research on raising, 162

stories, telling, importance of, 37, 93, 101, 140–141

strengths, celebrating, 21, 38, 46. *See also* celebration

structure, providing choice within, 23, 50. *See also* framework, for learning

students: acknowledging, 36, 69; advocacy for, 143; assessment of self-management by, 32; assuming intelligence of, 117; books written by, 45, 82–83; creating "need to know" in, 66–67; doing too much for far too long, 15; focusing on first, 17–18; getting to know, 11; meeting needs and interests of, 162; quality of discourse between, 35; relationships with, 21; schedules and needs of, 118; viewing classrooms through eyes of, 148–149. *See also* celebration; conferring with students; expectations of students

Suk Yoon, K., 133

summative assessment, defined, 138. *See also* assessment

summer reading programs, 83

sustained independent reading practice, 29–30, 82, 136. *See also* independent reading

T

Taylor, B., 82, 150

"teach less, learn more" motto, 85

teachers: as readers, 16, 47, 152; as writers, 57

Teacher Recognition Grant, ix

teaching: with efficiency, 144; extraordinary, 33; integrating arts into,

154–155; interruptions to, 94–95; joy of, 68–69; knowledgeable teachers, 3, 14, 16, 84, 89, 128, 162, 163; seamless, aiming for, 106; with sense of urgency, 77; telling compared to responsive teaching, 66, 150; to test, 88–89, 150; viewing celebration as, 111; whole-part-whole, 64, 101–102, 140

Teaching Essentials (Routman), 80

team leaders, 122

technology, wise use of, 71–72

TED talks websites, 160

testing: national obsession with, 68; teaching to test, 88–89, 150

texts: availability of, 44; bilingual, 141; choosing and using, 61, 158; complex, 61, 135–136, 152–153; exemplary, as models, 44; highlighting features of words in, 52; informational, 7, 49, 152–153; for reading aloud, 42; reading and writing authentic and continuous, 82–83; student-authored texts as reading texts, 141. *See also* books; shared writing

thinking, critical, 49, 67

thinking aloud for reading, writing, creating, and problem solving, 19

Transforming Our Teaching Through Reading to Understand (Routman), 158

Transforming Our Teaching Through Writing for Audience and Purpose (Routman), 8

Transitions: From Literature to Literacy (Routman), 1–2

tree house/tea house, 14, 53

truth, telling, 115–116

"turn and talk" time, 34, 50, 129, 141

tutorials, creating, 72

U–V

Unlikely Friendships (Holland), 58, 93

universal instruction: first level for all students, 117; as goal, 24

urgency, teaching with sense of, 77

Valencia, S.W., 151

values: persistence and effort, 36–37; uncertainty, 66–67

vertical teams, 131

visual arts, integrating, 154–155

vocabulary: integrating study of across curriculum, 51–52; making assumptions about, 62–63; nurturing development of, 107–108. *See also* word study; word walls

voices, encouraging all, 109

W

website of author: content available on, ix; "I Can Do It!" booklist, 93; blog posts, 47, 103; "View Success Story", 40

websites: classroom, school, and district, 71; edutopia.org, 72; ReadWriteThink. org, 72; TED talks, 160. *See also* social media sites; website of author

whiteboards, uses of, 51

whole-part-whole teaching, 64, 101–102, 140

word study, integration of across curriculum, 51–52

word walls: appearance of, 9; in content areas, 51, 108; feedback on, 80

writing: across curriculum, 49; authentic and continuous texts, 82–83; for authentic audiences and purposes, 8, 150; connecting with reading, 30, 41, 44–45; editing work, 86–87; effective, 18; explaining posted, 10; focusing on writers first, 38–39; handwriting, 96; posted, 131–132; public conferences about, 78–79; for readers, 86; rereading as part of, 27; revising drafts, 27, 98; "right" texts for, 61; shared writing, 109–110; short writing assignments, 70; stamina for, building, 147

writing conferences. *See* conferring with students; public writing conferences

Writing Essentials (Routman), 70, 109